Learn Ruby on Rails
For
Web Development

By: John Elder
Codemy.com

Learn Ruby on Rails For Web Development

By: John Elder

Published By Codemy.com
Chicago, IL USA

ISBN
978-0-692-36421-5

First Edition

TABLE OF CONTENTS

ABOUT THE AUTHOR

John Elder is a Web Developer, Entrepreneur, and Author living in Chicago, IL. He created one of the earliest online advertising networks in the late nineties and sold it to publicly traded WebQuest International Inc at the height of the first dot-com boom.

He went on to develop one of the Internet's first Search Engine Optimization tools, the Submission-Spider that was used by over three million individuals, small businesses, and governments in over forty-two countries.

These days John does freelance web development work, writes about Programming, Growth Hacking, and Internet Advertising, and runs **Codemy.com** the online school that teaches coding, Internet Marketing, and entrepreneurship to thousands of students.

John graduated with honors from Washington University in St. Louis with a degree in Economics. He can be reached at john@codemy.com

INTRODUCTION

"Rails? What a bloated waste of time...I'll NEVER use it for anything...ever."

That was really the first thought I had about Rails when I first looked into using it almost a decade ago. I'm an old school PHP guy who always built websites by simply punching out HTML and PHP onto Windows Notepad by hand, saving the file and uploading it to my regular apache web server using basic FTP software.

Compared to that, Rails seemed like a massive and unnecessary sort of thing. Who needs a whole big framework just to build a simple website?

And talk about complicated! The first time I tried to install Rails, I gave up in complete frustration after about an hour and a half.

Compared to hand-coding some HTML and PHP on notepad and then FTP'ing it up to my server, this Rails thing seemed borderline insane! In fact, it wasn't till recently that I even bothered to check out Rails again, and I'm glad I did because once you get past the insanity that is Rails installation...Rails is a *dream* to use!

It's just...fun!

You can do so much with Rails, so quickly, that it makes anything else seem crazy by comparison...even basic PHP.

It's true, there's a bit of a learning curve...in fact, it's unnecessarily hard to get started using Rails in the beginning unless you have someone to guide you through it (that's where this book comes into play). But once you get past a few initial rough patches, Rails is really quite easy...and I've been there so I can ease you through those initial bumps along the way.

In fact, I think you'll be surprised just how quickly you'll be building apps…

SO WHAT EXACTLY IS RUBY ON RAILS?

Ruby on Rails is an open source web development framework written in the Ruby programming language that makes creating apps and websites incredibly easy.

It uses something called a model/view/controller architecture that does a lot of the dirty work of dealing with databases and things like that for you, allowing you to focus on what's important to develop your app with speed and ease.

It was created by David Heinemeier Hansson back around 2004 - 2005 ish and quickly became one of the most popular app frameworks in the world. Many popular sites use it, including Groupon, Indiegogo, Airbnb, Yammer, SoundCloud, Scribd, Shopify, Hulu and many many others. Twitter was initially developed using Rails. Yep.

WHO IS THIS BOOK FOR?

This book is for the absolute Rails beginner. You don't need to have any prior experience with Rails whatsoever. It'll be helpful if you have some web development experience of some sort (a basic understanding of HTML is a plus, Javascript is a plus too) but you certainly don't need to know anything at all to get started with this book.

I'll walk you through absolutely everything you need to know step by step.

DO YOU NEED TO LEARN THE RUBY PROGRAMMING LANGUAGE?

The first thing that most people tend to ask me is whether or not you need to learn the Ruby programming language to use Rails. Though it is called *Ruby* on Rails, you don't really need to know Ruby to start using Rails to develop web apps.

We'll be using some simple embedded Ruby along the way (embedded Ruby is just Ruby that's used on a web page...*embedded* on a web page), but it'll be very basic Ruby and I'll walk you through it.

If you have any experience with other programming languages, you'll be able to pick up Ruby pretty easily. There are lots of free resources online that will teach you the basics. In fact, I'm finishing up a book on basic Ruby at the moment that you can check out if you're interested in learning more.

WHAT WILL WE MAKE IN THIS BOOK?

No one wants to read boring dry instructions. That's a fairly terrible way to learn anything! Instead we'll spend most of this book actually building an app from start to finish.

In this case, we'll be building a clone of **Pinterest**. Why Pinterest? Lots of reasons, really. Pinterest is one of the most popular websites on the Internet, it'll allow us cover a broad range of topics that you'll be able to use forever in whatever app/website that you work on in the future. It'll teach us how to create users, log them in and out of our app, allow them to upload text and images to a database, and then stylize all that stuff onto a webpage using some neat effects.

Plus, I think you'll discover that building Pinterest is pretty easy! Hopefully that realization will give you the confidence to strike out and build your own cool stuff.

If a site like Pinterest is *this* easy to create, well, you can probably build just about anything!

HOW DO YOU LEARN?

Some people learn best by reading, others learn by watching or listening...still others learn by using their hands and actually *do-ing* things. It's my goal to tick as many of those boxes as possible to give you the tools you need to really learn Rails quickly and easily in whatever method of learning works best for you.

So in addition to this book, I've also created an online video course that follows along with the book. You can actually watch me complete each of the steps in the book and build our clone of Pinterest right in front of your eyes.

You can ask me questions online if you get stuck along the way, and hang out with everyone else who's enrolled in the course on the course message board.

The video course is hosted at the online code school, Codemy.com and you can follow along and watch at your own pace.

We've got a lot of different courses besides this rails course. If you're interested in learning Internet Marketing, Web Development, or how to build an online Startup I highly recommend you check Codemy.com out. People are actually raving about it, which is pretty cool!

Full Membership gets you access to all the courses for just $497, or you can sign up for individual video courses (like this Rails course) for just $97 each.

As a thank you for reading this book, I'd like to offer you $22 off the Rails course (get it for just $75). Just use coupon code **amazon** when you order from:

http://www.Codemy.com/rails/

CONVENTIONS USED THROUGHOUT THE BOOK

This is a book about computer programming, so the layout is a little bit different than your average work of fiction (or non-fiction for that matter).

First let's talk terminology.

I won't use a lot of weird technical terms...and if I do I'll be sure to explain them.

One thing I want to mention is my use of the term 'app'. Most people use the phrase 'app' when talking about anything made online these days, and especially anything created using Rails.

I tend to use the phrase 'website' instead of 'app'. I guess technically a website is just an App...and Rails will build an 'App' directory...but what can I say...I'm weird I guess. To me a website is a website...so I tend to call them websites.

So just sort of be aware that I'll generally slip between the phrase 'app' and 'website' interchangeably when I get excited. You should probably emulate the cool kidz and just call them apps.

I'll be writing a lot of code in this book, and I'll usually designate that code by displaying it in big grey boxes as per the regular convention to list code in big grey boxes. That should make it easier to read and less jumbled with the rest of the text of the book.

Unfortunately, Kindle books don't generally show those big grey boxes, the formatting they use tends to strip that sort of thing out. In that case, hopefully the code will show up in a numbered list. Each number represents a line of code, sort of like this:

```
1    < if user_logged_in? do %>
2       something here
3    <% else %>
4       Do something else
5    <% end %>
```

Everyone who signs up for my Ruby on Rails course over at Codemy.com will get a pdf version of this book for free, and that pdf has code listed with the traditional grey boxes which I think makes everything easier to differentiate.

Finally, we'll be using something called the "command line", sometimes called the "terminal" extensively throughout this book (and in everyday Rails life).

If you aren't familiar with the command line, don't worry, I'll explain it in a moment. But for now, just understand that when I write command line commands, I'll also be writing them in the same sort of big grey boxes that I display code in.

Normally a rails app will be deep in a unix-style directory, like this: /home/ubuntu/workspace/your_rails_app/

And the command line convention is to put the name of your computer/user before that directory structure. So your command line might look something like this:

Elder-laptop: /home/ubuntu/workspace/your_rails_app/ $

That dollar sign "$" is the command prompt.

I'm not going to type all that stuff out every time I tell you to type a command line command. Instead I'll generally just write the dollar sign and the command, and you should assume that command should be typed into the directory where you Rails app is sitting. So it might look something like this:

$ rake db:migrate

Which means; in the directory /home/ubuntu/workspace/your_rails_app/ type the rake db:migrate command.

But like the grey box problem I just mentioned a second ago with our code snippets, Kindle is going to strip out the grey box for my command line examples, so I'll also use the numbered method like the code snippets, like so:

```
1  $ rake db:migrate
2
```

Cool?

Cool.

CHAPTER ONE

THE DEVELOPMENT ENVIRONMENT

The first time I tried to install Rails and all the stuff that goes along with it, I gave up in sheer frustration after more than an hour of hair-pulling exasperation.

I've been programming computers since I was seven years old. I think it's safe to say that trying to install Rails for the first time was by far the most mind-numbing, unclear, obscure, bottomless pit of insanity that I've ever encountered in the world of programming.

Even today; installing Rails seems to take me over a half hour, and if I'm not paying particularly close attention, something STILL goes wrong. It's just bizarre! I think that's a real shame because it definitely turns away a lot of people from learning Rails.

And it's all so...*un-necessary!*

First things first, in a traditional Rails installation, the type of computer operating system you're running will determine how you install Rails (and Ruby too...don't forget about Ruby - it needs to be installed as well!).

Basically we're looking at three options here. Either you're running a Windows machine of some sort, a Mac, or some flavor of Linux.

Traditionally, Rails developers tend to use Macs or Linux operating systems because those both have command line terminals built right in and both run on a traditional Unix directory structure.

There's a Windows version of Rails that you can install if you're determined to use a Windows PC but that's a whole can of insanity that I'm not willing to open, let alone swallow.

If you simply *must* use a Windows PC as your development tool of choice, don't use the Windows version of Rails. Instead, I highly suggest that you download the free VirtualBox software from Oracle (**https://www.virtualbox.org/**) and install a Linux virtual machine on your computer. I suggest you choose Ubuntu for your Linux OS (it's free, really popular, and fun to use).

BUT!! We aren't going to go the traditional route in this book! We aren't going to install Rails at all! You my friend, are living in a golden age where development environments can be run IN THE CLOUD!

So it doesn't matter if you're running a Windows PC, a Mac, or a Linux box...we'll all log into a virtual environment way up there in the magic cloud that has everything we need pre-installed and just waiting for us to play with.

There are a lot of cloud development companies to choose from, most of them offer free tiers that are more than powerful enough for our purposes (most allow free environments for single developers - you usually just have to pay for multi-user accounts when you have lots of team members that need to access the thing all at once).

A couple popular choices are:

http://nitrous.io
http://c9.io

For this book we're going to use http://c9.io

So head over there and sign up for a free account. Just enter your email address and pick a password, then verify your email address by clicking the link in the email that they auto-send you and you're good to go.

When you log into your account you'll see your user dashboard:

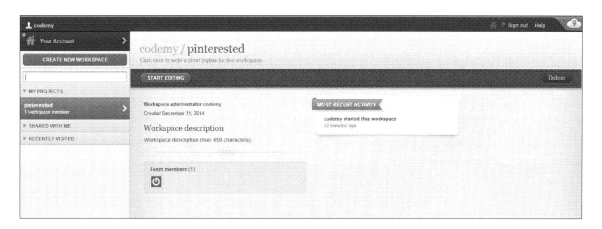

(C9.io Dashboard)

Up at the top left-hand corner of the screen; click the button that says "Create New Workspace". A Workspace is what c9.io calls the development environment. You'll create a new workspace for every Rails App that you build. Since we're just building one app in this book, we just need one workspace.

From the box that pops up, name your new Rails app, let's call ours: pinterested. Type that into the field that asks for the name, click the "Ruby on Rails" icon to designate that this will be a ruby app, and then click the "Create" button.

That's all there is to it! In a few moments (sometimes up to a minute), your Rails development environment will be ready to go!

One of the nice things about these cloud environments is that you can access them from anywhere, on any computer that has a web browser and an Internet connection. It doesn't matter if you're on a Windows, a Mac, or a Linux machine. And it will always be exactly how you left it.

I guess there's nothing left to do but fire up our new dev environment and see what's what!

(C9.io Development Environment)

So let's take a quick look at what we've got here. Basically there are three sections. The section on the left sidebar is a list of directories and files that come with Rails. These are the standard directories and files that come with ALL Rails installations.

There's a lot of stuff there and it might seem overwhelming at first. That's OK! I'm going to break it all down and explain what's important for us to know about, and what we can ignore for later (and what we can ignore forever).

The next section is the sort of lower middle section.

That's the command line. Some people call it the terminal (if you're on a Mac or Linux and not using a cloud development environment, you'll use an actual terminal that will look and act similar to this one). The terminal, or command line (I tend to use each of those terms interchangeably), is where we'll type in commands to do a lot of different things along the way.

The section right above that, which should have some sort of readme document open the first time, is basically the text editor. It allows us to open files, edit files, and save files. We'll be spending a big chunk of our time using the text editor.

You can close that readme file and any other welcome page type files that are open. Just click the little X at the top of each file in the text editor.

To open one of the files from the directory tree on the left hand side of the screen, just double click it and it should open in the text editor.

WHAT VERSION OF RAILS AND RUBY ARE WE USING?

Normally if we were running our development environment on a Mac, Linux, or Windows PC, you would usually need to update the version of both Ruby and Rails on your system. We don't really need to worry about that in this case because we're working on a cloud development environment and usually they keep these things fairly up to date.

But I might as well show you how to check and see which version of both Ruby and Rails we're currently running. It may be the case in the future when you need to run specific versions of Ruby or Rails or something else, so being able to figure out what version you're running is important. It also let's gain a little familiarity with the terminal.

So head down to the terminal and type in:

```
1 $ rails -v
2
```

It should output something like:

```
1  $ rails -v
2  Rails 4.1.6
3
```

So that means that we are currently running Rails version 4.1.6. That's ok. As of the writing of this book, there's a newer version of Rails out; 4.2.0 but we don't really need to update.

Next go ahead and check the version of Ruby that we're currently running. Can you guess what command we'll need to type in? Shockingly enough, it's:

```
1  $ ruby -v
2
```

And that should output something like this:

```
1  $ ruby -v
2  ruby 2.1.4p265
3
```

Which means that we're running Ruby version 2.1.4p265. Likewise, that's a new enough version of Ruby to suit our purposes.

COMMON TERMINAL COMMANDS

So that's how the terminal works; you just enter commands and hit enter and the command gets executed, and then there's usually some sort of output that you can see. The terminal is actually a pretty powerful device and you can do a ton of things with it.

Of courses, in this book we won't be diving too deep into the wonderful world of command line goodness, but it's probably helpful to go over a few common commands that we might come across as we go along. So let's take a quick look at some common command line commands.

```
1  $ pwd
2
```

The pwd command shows us what directory we're currently in. When I type it into my terminal, I get this:

```
1  $ pwd
2  /home/ubuntu/workspace
3
```

That means that we are currently in the home/ubuntu/workspace directory. The workspace directory contains all of the files and directories that we see listed over there on the left hand side of the screen. In fact, we can see exactly what files are included in that directory (or any directory for that matter) by entering the ls command:

```
1  $ ls
2
```

That will output something that looks like this:

```
1  $ ls
2  Gemfile Gemfile.lock README.md README.rdoc Rakefile app/ bin/
3  config/ config.ru db/ lib/ log/ public/ spring/ test/ tmp/ vendor/
4
```

The things with slashes next to them (' / ') are directories, the rest are files.

We can navigate to those directories by using the cd command. cd stands for "change directory" and looks like this:

```
1  $ cd public/
2
```

That will move us into the public directory. Running the pwd command will now show us:

```
1  $ pwd
2  /home/ubuntu/workspace/public
3
```

To move back to our workspace directory, we can issue this command:

```
1  $ cd ../
2
```

Which basically says "move backwards one level"...and now we find ourselves back in the workspace directory.

Here's a fun fact tip about the cd command...you don't have to actually type out the entire command. Usually you can just start to type in out and then hit your 'tab' key on the keyboard and the terminal will autocorrect fill in the rest of the thing. So if you type in cd pu and then hit tab, it will fill the rest in (cd public/) and then you can just hit enter.

That might not seem like such a big deal, but sometimes you can end up typing a long bunch of words into the command line, using that tab trick really helps!

CREATING YOUR FIRST RAILS PROJECT

Normally if we weren't running a virtual development environment, we'd have to generate our new rails project. You'd do that by navigating to the directory where you'd like to create your app (in our case it would be the 'workspace' directory) and then enter this command:

```
1  $ rails new pinterested
2
```

That command would generate a new project called pinterested and place it into the workspaces directory. Fortunately we don't have to do that in this case because we're working on a virtual development environment and c9.io spins up our new project when we first create it on the c9.io dashboard.

So we're already good to go. Those new project files have already been generated; in fact, those are the files that you see listed in the directory tree on the left hand side of your screen, or by entering the command: ls in the command line.

FIRING UP OUR APP

So all of the files are there, but in order to first fire up our app we need to start up the Rails server. Out of the box, Rails comes with a lightweight web server called WEBrick. It isn't really production level quality, but it works just fine in our development environment. Normally you'd want something like Apache or

Nginx for your production web server, and we'll talk about that later. For now, we're happy to use WEBrick.

To fire up our WEBrick server, just click that button at the very top of the screen, right in the middle of the screen, that says 'Run Project'.

If we were working on a mac/linux/winpc, we would need to enter this command into the terminal (in the same directory where our project is located):

1 $ rails server
2

But since we're on a cloud development environment, we can just click the Run Project button at the top of the screen.

You'll notice that when we click that button, a new terminal box pops up. The WEBRick server is running in that terminal, and we can switch back and forth between those two terminal screens. Once the web server starts running, it keeps running in that terminal and you won't be able to do anything else in that terminal (that's why a new terminal screen popped up).

Take a look at that terminal, you should see a line at the very top that says something like:

1 Your code is running at **https://pinterested-codemy.c9.io**.
2 => Booting WEBrick
3 …

...and then a whole bunch of other stuff. Give it a few moments to get up and running and then type that URL into a new tab on your web browser (be sure to remove the period that's oddly listed at the end of the URL).

That should bring up a screen that looks like this:

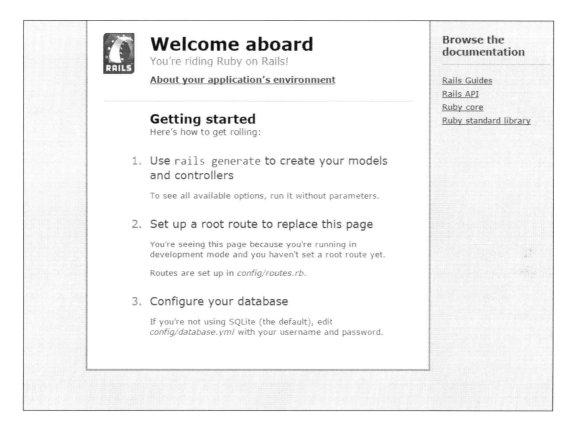

(Default Rails Project Homepage)

Congratulations! You've officially created your very first Rails app. Sure, there's not really much of anything there at the moment, but we can quickly change that!

Before we add more pages, I want to take a couple of minutes to explain the architecture that Rails uses… it's called the MVC architecture.

UNDERSTANDING THE MVC ARCHITECTURE

MVC stands for Model, View, Controller and it allows us to separate the different parts of our web app and only need to focus on the things that are most important to us. That'll make more sense in just a few moments, I promise!

So let's take a quick look at each of these things.

MODEL: the model is basically the database.

VIEW: the views are basically the web pages, think of them as the thing that people see (or VIEW) when they go to your web site.

CONTROLLER: the controller is the thing that sits behind the scenes and 'controls' the interaction between the web page VIEW and the database MODEL. Think of the controller as an air flight traffic controller, telling things where to go and generally controlling everything.

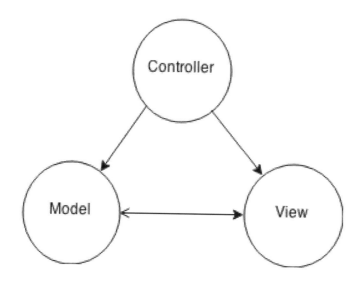

(Model View Controller Diagram)

So our rails app is made up of these three different areas, and if you browse through that directory tree on the left hand side of the screen (specifically look in the 'app' directory), you'll see things like views, models, and controllers. Looking around a bit more you'll see a db directory.

We don't need to know what all of these things are or what they do just yet; we just need to start familiarizing ourselves with the fact that those things are there, and that they correspond to something in either the MODEL, VIEW, or CONTROLLER part of our MCV framework.

Why is this cool?

It probably makes very little sense right now, but the MVC architecture is VERY cool because it lets us focus on the things we really care about, like the Views (how our website looks) and can sit back and let Rails itself (through the behind the scenes controllers) deal with the nitty gritty nasty database stuff.

I've been programming computers since I was seven years old. But to this day databases still give me headaches. I understand how they work, I know how to use them, and I HAVE used them hundreds of times in the past...but I don't *like* using them! I always have to look things up, I always tend to screw something up, and generally I just have bad experiences with databases.

Rails is fantastic because I don't have to deal with any database junk...Rails does all the heavy lifting for me! I just have to tell Rails "hey create a table with these columns that will contain this type of data" and Rails does the rest. This will make more sense as we move along, so you'll have to just trust me for now!

GEMFILES

Besides the MVC architecture, the other main component of Rails that you need to be aware of, are things called Gems.

Gems are really cool. In fact, Gems are what allows us to build really cool apps very *very* quickly. Whenever you want to do something interesting or complicated but don't want to write the code to do it yourself (which is pretty much EVERY time – right?) you simply add a Gem.

Gems add functionality to our apps. Pretty much any functionality you'd like to add, you can find a Gem to use.

Want users to be able to join your site, log in, log out, and update their user info? Writing the code to do that would take a LOT of work and experience. Instead, slap in a Gem.

Want users to be able to upload images to your site? Slap in the paperclip gem.

You get the idea.

We'll be using lots of Gems in this book and you'll get used to adding and installing them. For right now, I just want to introduce you to the concept.

RubyGems.org is the worldwide repository of Gems. That's where you can search for specific Gems and read the documentation for each of them. Some Gems are well documented, some are not.

I don't know how many Gems there are, but as of today those Gems have been downloaded 4,185,990,468 times...that's over four billion. So, yeah!

Adding Gems to your project is generally pretty easy, and I don't want you to get hung up on this process because it'll become old hat later on. For now I'll just outline the basic process.

Your app contains a file, called the Gemfile where you'll type in all the Gems you'll be using. You can see the Gemfile there on the left-hand side of your development environment towards the bottom of the list of files. Open it now by clicking it.

(Gemfile)

You'll see that there are Gems listed in there already. Rails installed them automatically when you started your project. Let's go ahead and clean that file up a bit.

Normally we like to use comments (those lines that start with '#') because it helps explain our code. But in this case those comments are just in the way.

So delete all the comments and straighten up the file a bit.

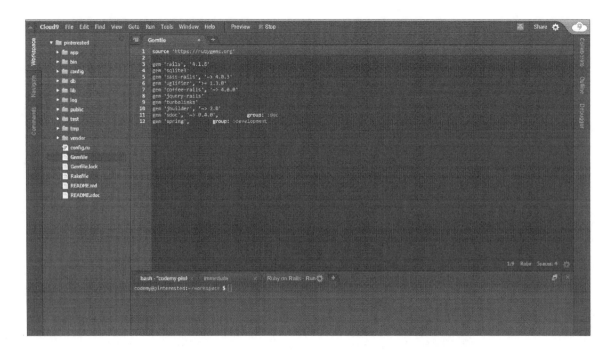

(Cleaned Up Gemfile With No Comments)

So that's our Gemfile. To add a new Gem, we just type in the name of the Gem and it's version number on a new line in the Gemfile. Then in the terminal you'll type in the command:

```
1 $ bundle install
2
```

That will install all of the Gems that have been added since the last time you ran the bundle install command. Generally it's a good idea to close your Rails Server terminal and restart your rails app as well after every bundle install.

I always forget to restart my Rails server and so I usually get an error when I reload a web page after installing a Gem. Then I smack my head and remember to restart the server and everything works out ok.

Some Gems only require you to add their name and version number to the Gemfile and then run the bundle install command. Other Gems may have special instructions that are a little more elaborate. Each Gem's documentation will tell you how to install it specifically, and usually how to use the Gem in your app.

But we'll get into all that later. As we move throughout this book building our Pinterested app, adding Gems will become old hat.

ADDING PAGES TO OUR WEB APPLICATION

So enough MVC theory jibber jabber, let's add some pages to our app. Head back to our development environment and pull up the main terminal (not the one still running the web server). Next type this command into the command prompt.

```
1  $ rails generate controller home index
2
```

So what does this line do? It tells our Rails app to add a new page called index, and to add that page to the home directory and generate a controller for it. Typing that command in should result in this bunch of gobbledigook:

```
1   create  app/controllers/home_controller.rb
2   route   get 'home/index'
3   invoke  erb
4   create    app/views/home
5   create    app/views/home/index.html.erb
6   invoke  test_unit
7   create    test/controllers/home_controller_test.rb
8   invoke  helper
9   create    app/helpers/home_helper.rb
10  invoke    test_unit
11  create      test/helpers/home_helper_test.rb
12  invoke  assets
13  invoke    coffee
14  create      app/assets/javascripts/home.js.coffee
15  invoke    scss
16  create      app/assets/stylesheets/home.css.scss
```

So that's a whole lot of stuff! Right now, we don't *really* need to know what all that stuff is. For now, just understand that we've generated a new controller, and a new page called index that's sitting in the home directory. In fact, we can switch over to our running app in the next browser tab and type in:

https://pinterested-codemy.c9.io/home/index

Be sure to replace the 'codemy' with whatever your account name is at c9.io, and be sure to change the pinterested to whatever you named your project (wait - didn't you name your project pinterested? Of course you did!).

Here's what you should see if everything went according to plan:

Home#index

Find me in app/views/home/index.html.erb

(Rails initial /home/index page: https://pinterested-codemy.c9.io/home/index)

Sure, there's not much on that page yet...but how easy was it to create? Pretty easy. Now we can edit that page and make it look however we want.

So where exactly IS that file? It's located at:

```
1  /home/ubuntu/workspace/app/views/home/index.html.erb
2
```

That's where it is located via the command line, but there's no reason for us to navigate to that file via the command line. Instead we can just double-click through the directory tree sitting right there on the left hand side of the screen.

Double-click the app directory to expand it, then double-click the views directory to expand it, then double-click the home directory to expand it, and voila! You should see the index.html.erb file sitting right there. Go ahead and double-click it and it should fire right up in the text editor there in the middle of the screen.

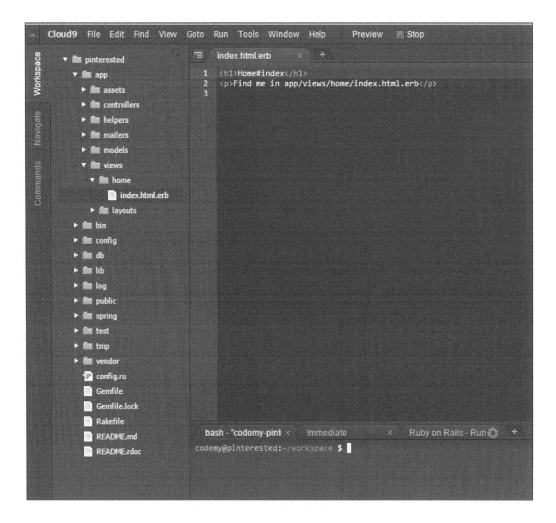

(Development Environment Directory Tree /app/views/home/index.html.erb)

NOTE: notice how the file ends in .erb? Most web pages tend to end in .html but our Rails pages tend to end in .html.erb and that tells the app to allow us to use embedded Ruby (.erb) on each web page. We'll look at embedded Ruby soon.

Take a look at our index.html.erb file in text editor (shown above):

```
1  <h1>Home#index</h1>
2  <p>Find me in app/views/home/index.html.erb</p>
3
```

Again...there's not much there right now, but we can edit it and make it look however we want just by editing it in the text editor right now.

So let's edit that index.html.erb file. Fire it up in the text editor and replace what's there already with this, or whatever you like:

```
1  <h1>Welcome To My App</h1>
2  <p>It's Gonna Kick All Ass...</p>
```

Then go ahead and save it by hitting Control and S (Ctrl + S) and your keyboard, or command S if you're running a Mac.

Now head back to that page in your web browsers and hit reload on your browser.

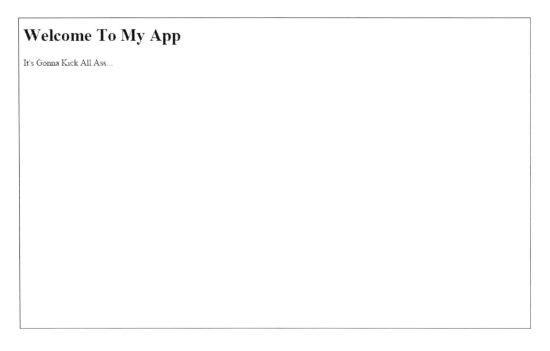

Welcome To My App

It's Gonna Kick All Ass...

(Updated rails /home/index page: https://pinterested-codemy.c9.io/home/index)

See how easy that was? Sure there's still not much there, and we didn't really do anything with that edit...but it's going to come quickly now!

CHANGE THE ROUTE

We've touched on MVC a little bit, now let's see a little bit of it in action. Right now our Index page is located at **https://pinterested-codemy.c9.io/home/index**

But what we'd really like to see is that page shown as our main homepage at **https://pinterested-codemy.c9.io** So how do we do that?

Easily.

All we need to do is change the routing of our project a bit (think controller in the MVC). Take a look at /config/routes.rb

/config/routes.rb
1 Rails.application.routes.draw do
2 get 'home/index'
3 .
4 .
5 end
6

Navigate to that file in the directory tree on the left side of the screen of your development environment and double click it to open it in the text editor. You should see a couple lines at the top of that file, and then a page full of commented out stuff (stuff with #'s in front of it).

So what's going on here? Basically that file is telling our app to route our index.html.erb file to home/index and that's why our index page shows up at:

https://pinterested-codemy.c9.io/home/index

In fact, in the future if we want to add more pages, we'll have to add routes to those pages right here. They'll probably look a lot like that line (get 'home/index') only for different pages (ie get 'home/about' would create a route to a page at /home/about etc).

But for now we need to modify that line to let our program know that we don't want our index page routed to /home/index. In fact, we want to make that our ROOT page (ie the page at the root of our url **https://pinterested-codemy.c9.io**), Easy enough, just edit that file:

/config/routes.rb

```
1  Rails.application.routes.draw do
2  root 'home#index'
3  .
4  .
5  end
6
```

See what we did? We changed the line get 'home/index' into the line root 'home#index'

Notice the '#' instead of a '/', that's what we need to do to designate that page as a root page. If we go ahead and save the newly edited routes.rb file and reload our web browser at **https://pinterested-codemy.c9.io/home/index** we'll get an error because the route to that page no longer exists!

Instead if we navigate to **https://pinterested-codemy.c9.io** we'll see our index page right there, which is exactly what we were shooting for.

Things are moving right along! We better save our work!

VERSION CONTROL WITH GITHUB AND BITBUCKET

One of the most important things to do as a programmer is set up version control to keep track of all the different changes you make as you develop your app. It's generally a 'best-practices' type of thing, but it makes sense.

If you totally blow up your app (and you probably will at some point), it's nice to be able to simply roll back to before you blew it up and proceed ahead as if nothing happened.

Version control is especially useful when you're working with a bunch of people, and they're all making changes and adding/removing things. Your version control will keep track of who did what, and when and where.

But it's important even if you're working by yourself and don't plan on ever working with a team of people because you're always going to screw up and need to roll back your code. Trust me.

Most coders use something called "Git" for their version control, and then push their code up to a third party website like Github or Bitbucket for safe keeping.

You have a choice when it comes to picking a third party site to host your code on. Github seems to be much more popular, all the coders seem to use it. In fact, most people use their Github account as a sort of resume piece.

Why? Because unless you pay for it, all the code you push up to Github is public. Anyone can see it, download it, whatever. So potential employers always want to see your Github account; so they can check out your chops.

That's fine if you're working on a lot of open source type projects, but personally I'm usually developing proprietary apps that I'm using to make me money. I don't want ANYONE to see that code.

So I use Bitbucket. Bitbucket gives you free private repositories, and you only have to pay to add team members and things like that. But for individuals, you get free private repositories. Github, on the other hand, gives you free PUBLIC repositories and you pay to get private ones.

I think it's a good idea to have some sort of Github presence if you're looking to turn this programming thing into a full time job. Like I said, employers will want to see your Github page.

What I recommend you do is use Github for things like this book! As you follow along with the code in this book (and any others you read) use Github.

We're building a pinterest clone. Another book might show you to make a shopping cart like site. Still another book might teach you to clone Twitter.

If you follow along with each of those books building what they build, at the end you'll have three solid example projects on your Github page to show potential employers. And then they'll hire you for hundreds of thousands of dollars a year in salary and you can send me some of that cash every month :-p

So it just depends on what you're doing whether or not you use Github or Bitbucket. I'll show you how to set up each of them right now.

INSTALLING GIT

Normally you'd need to install git into your development environment, but we're using the awesome c9.io cloud environment and they've already installed git for us and it's ready to go.

All we need to do is configure it. So let's do that now. We've got to punch in four or five commands into our terminal command line:

1   $ git config --global user.name "Your Name"
2   $ git config --global user.email **your.email@example.com**
3   $ git config --global push.default matching
4   $ git config --global alias.co checkout
5   $ git init
6

So obviously you're going to want to change line 1 to add your own name where it says "Your Name" and just as obviously you're going to want to add your actual email address to line to where it asks for your email address.

Remember, Git is used to keep track of who makes what changes, so it needs to know your name and email address.

You'll have noticed that after you entered the last command (line 5) you got a little output printed on the screen; probably something like this:

```
1  $ git init
2  Initialized empty Git repository in /home/ubuntu/workspace/.git/
3
```

Basically that means that a new directory has been generated to handle all of our version control files on our development environment, and that directory is named .git/ You can cd into that directory in the terminal if you're curious to see what's in there (just remember to cd ../ back to the main directory when you're done snooping around).

So now Git is configured for our development environment, we need to add our project files to our local repository. Once we've added them, we'll 'push' them up to either Github or Bitbucket. Adding our project files to our local git repository is a two-step process:

```
1  $ git add .
2
```

That command will add all the files of our project into a sort of staging area. Basically it says "Hey, my files are ready to go!" The period '.' means "all files". Next we need to 'commit' those files to the repository. Committing, in essence, moves the files from the staging area into the repository.

```
1  $ git commit -am "initial commit"
2
```

There's a couple of things to notice with this command. First the flag -am. That tells git to grab all (-a) our staged files and look for a comment (technically a 'message' hence the -m flag). The comment is "initial commit". You can type anything you want as the comment, just enclose it in either a double quote or single quote.

Comments are important for version control because the comment/message will be shown next to every file that has changed since the last commit. That makes it easier to eyeball your code up on Github or Bitbucket and track down specific changes.

So for instance, let's pretend we just added an 'about us' page to our project and wanted to commit the changes. In that case I would have typed $ git commit -am "added an about us page"

That's how comments/messages work in version control. Get used to typing those two lines, followed by a third line to push the code up to github or bitbucket that we'll look at in a minute.

ROLLING BACK CODE

So now if you make some catastrophic mistake, you can roll your code back (as long as you haven't committed the mistaken code already). All you have to do is punch in this command:

```
1  $ git checkout -f
2
```

And your errors will melt away.

GITHUB OR BITBUCKET

So now and all we need to do now is decide whether or not to use Github or Bitbucket to host our code.

GitHub.com
Bitbucket.org

Head over to one or the other of those sites and sign up for a free account.

USING BITBUCKET

Like I said, I'll show you how to use both, but since I tend to use Bitbucket myself, we'll start with them.

After you sign up for a Bitbucket account, you'll need to add an SSH key so that Bitbucket knows you are who you say you are when you push code from your development environment onto your Bitbucket account.

Normally you'd have to generate a public key, but our development environment already has one ready to go, and you can find it by punching in this command to the terminal:

```
1  $ cat ~/.ssh/id_rsa.pub
2
```

That should output a whole bunch of gobblediegook to the screen that looks something like this:

ssh-rsa

AAAAB3NzaC1yc2EAAAADAQABAAABAQDg4sk2R4EigtmQ3WLuw03EFMN/
fNGkpOQ1hj/HdQ9SI0b/SdGpxK3z9Bz75UFDPCnhjvCNrcYiARzfTN1pqBOjKEq
74ZWoVtdwcpjhkePHDnBdVz2upnrgGCWu/BAs14oRhTsVIpZGtt/RsVe8OfsXsc+
lIpKGWUAMtg4hwORni6qeY845OWRrdeQLCpx5ZJDrzSeYNtGBx5oHEqAglOaB
TSS/aFewwcQe8WuXrWlrQy4C63Oas/+mLgYPhzjirN9eiHrKuRgj35jlv5jYoSK484h
BxxAPelia5yLf0grWG0j7hq4vyZM0QNyyKLh2LpURwzmM9b/Ur9hL7OMjGUbp
johne4196@gmail.com

That's your public SSH key. Drag your mouse over the whole lot of it to highlight it, and then copy it by pressing Control and C (Ctrl + C) or Command C on a Mac. Now we need to paste that into our Bitbucket account.

Log into your account and click the little avatar image at the top right corner of your dashboard screen, then click "Manage Account", and then click "SSH Keys".

A box should pop up where you can paste (Ctrl +V) your newly copied SSH key. Click the "Add Key" button after you've pasted the key into the appropriate box.

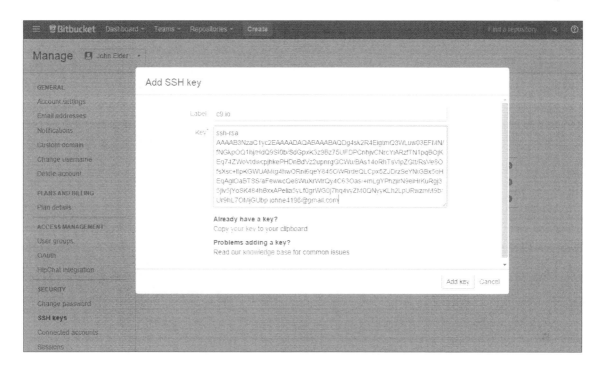

(Bitbucket.org Add SSH key screen)

So far so good. Now we need to create a new repository on Bitbucket. Click the "Create" link and type in the name of your app. You can generally leave the rest of the default fields alone.

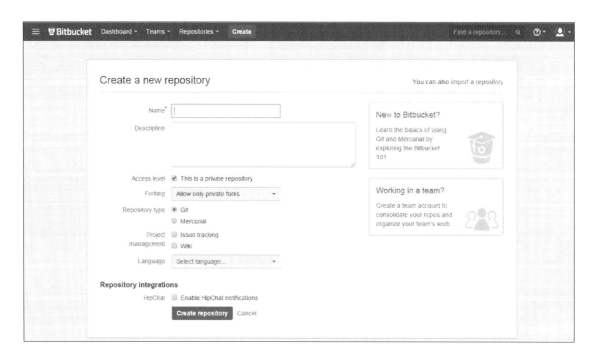

(Bitbucket.org Create Repository Screen)

Now we need to punch in a couple of commands into our terminal back at our c9.io development environment:

```
1  $ git remote add origin git@bitbucket.org:<username>/pinterested.git
2  $ git push -u origin --all
3
```

Be sure to change the <username> field to your Bitbucket username, and change the /pinterested.git name to whatever you actually named your app over at Bitbucket.

Done and done.

From now on, whenever you want to save your code and push it to Bitbucket, you'll follow these three commands:

1 $ git add .
2 $ git commit -am 'enter your comment'
3 $ git push
4

We've already seen the first two command, they add your files to your local git repository. It's the third line ($ git push) that actually pushes all that committed code up to Bitbucket.

And now we've got version control completely set up and ready to go!

USING GITHUB

Now we'll go over the steps for using Github. Remember, don't try to use BOTH of these services, you need to pick one or the other.

So the first thing to do is head over to Github.com and sign up for a free account.

After that you'll need to do the same basic steps we just went over for generating a public SSH key for bitbucket:

1 $ cat ~/.ssh/id_rsa.pub
2

That should output a whole bunch of gobblediegook to the screen that looks something like this:

ssh-rsa

AAAAB3NzaC1yc2EAAAADAQABAAABAQDg4sk2R4EigtmQ3WLuw03EFMN/
fNGkpOQ1hj/HdQ9SI0b/SdGpxK3z9Bz75UFDPCnhjvCNrcYiARzfTN1pqBOjKEq
74ZWoVtdwcpjhkePHDnBdVz2upnrgGCWu/BAs14oRhTsVIpZGtt/RsVe8OfsXsc+
lIpKGWUAMtg4hwORni6qeY845OWRrdeQLCpx5ZJDrzSeYNtGBx5oHEqAglOaB
TSS/aFewwcQe8WuXrWlrQy4C63Oas/+mLgYPhzjirN9eiHrKuRgj35jlv5jYoSK484h
BxxAPelia5yLf0grWG0j7hq4vyZM0QNyyKLh2LpURwzmM9b/Ur9hL7OMjGUbp
johne4196@gmail.com

That's your public SSH key. Drag your mouse over the whole lot of it to highlight it, then copy it by pressing Control and C (Ctrl + C) or Command C on a mac. Now we need to paste that into our Github account.

Log into your Github account and look around for a little gear icon at the top right hand corner of the page.

Under 'User Settings' click 'SSH Keys'. In the 'Title' field, name this thing...I'd name it c9.io pinterested or something like that. Then paste your SSH key into the 'Key' field and click the add button. You may have to confirm by entering your Github password.

Now you can test things out to make sure everything worked the way it's supposed to work. Pull up the terminal in our development environment and punch in this command:

```
1  $ ssh -T git@github.com
2
```

You'll probably see something like this:

1   The authenticity of host 'github.com (207.97.227.239)' can't be established.
2   RSA key fingerprint is 16:27:ac:a5:76:28:2d:36:63:1b:56:4d:eb:df:a6:48.
3   Are you sure you want to continue connecting (yes/no)?
4

That's what you're supposed to see. Type in yes and hit enter. You'll probably see this:

1   Hi username! You've successfully authenticated, but GitHub does not
2   provide shell access.
3

Success! Now we need to create a repository on Github to house your project.

Look for a plus sign ('+') up at the top right hand corner of the screen somewhere. Click it and then click 'New Repository'. Name your repository something short and memorable...like pinterested or something like that.

Next you need to decide whether to make your repository public or private. If you've set up a free account, then you'll need to pick 'public'.

Don't click "Select Initialize this repository with a README." because we've already run $ git init in our development environment.

Click 'Create Repository'.

Now head back to your terminal in our development environment and push your code up to Github:

1   $ git remote add origin git@github.com:[username]/[repository name].git
2   $ git push -u origin master

That should do it! Remember, whenever you want to save code and push to Github, you'll need to do these three steps:

```
1  $ git add .
2  $ git commit -am 'your comment here'
3  $ git push
4
```

And that's all there is to it!

HOSTING YOUR APP ON HEROKU

So we've got version control set up and running, now we need to talk about hosting your app. One of the great things about Ruby on Rails is Heroku, which is basically a web hosting service for Rails apps.

Normally when you deal with web hosting, you've got to manage servers at some level. Depending on how much horsepower you need, you might be responsible for most of the administration of your web server, including patching and updating the thing, all the way up to security. It can suck.

Heroku is different.

With Heroku, all you have to do is push your code up to Heroku in much the same way that we push it to Bitbucket or Github. In fact, it's just one line on the terminal.

Your code will get pushed to Heroku where it will be automatically installed, configured, and whatever other magic needs to be done to turn your code into a fully functioning website.

Bang zoom, you're done.

You don't have to worry about running a web server, patching software, scaling things, or security. And did I mention Heroku is free?

Yep.

Well...it's free at a basic level. They have a "Pay as you Grow" type of model. Heroku works off something they call a 'dyno', and you can get one dyno for each app you upload for free. One dyno is enough horsepower to get your site up and running, and allow a handful of people to use your app at once.

The more people that use your app at once, the more horsepower and bandwidth you'll need. You'll need to increase the dynos for your app. That's pretty cool, because there's nothing to it. You just log into your account and increase the dynos.

So with the click of a button you can basically scale your website to be as powerful as you want; to handle as much traffic as you want. So basically you only pay for what you need, horsepower wise. That's great for new sites just getting started. As your web app becomes more popular and more people flood to your site, you just increase the dynos to the appropriate level.

Done and done.

It's a great resource, and fairly unique in the world of web hosting. What about price? Right now two dynos will cost you around $35-36 bucks a month. Three dynos will cost around $70 a month. You can check for yourself here:

https://www.heroku.com/pricing

There's a slider on that page that lets you see how much any level of dynos will cost per month and you can do your own research there.

There are certainly other hosting services where you can host your Rails app, but I've never bothered to research any of them. Heroku is the industry leader.

So sign up for a free Heroku account right now, and let's configure our app for Heroku.

Normally, if we were running our development environment on mac/windows/linux, we'd have to download and install the Heroku toolbelt (toolbelt.heroku.com).

But since we're using a virtual cloud development environment, we've already got the toolbelt installed. You can check to make sure by punching in this command into the terminal:

```
1  $ heroku --version
2
```

You should see a line output that tells you what version of the Heroku toolbelt is installed.

Now all we have to do is log into Heroku from the terminal:

```
1  $ heroku login
2
```

You'll be prompted to enter your email address and password right there on the command line. Go ahead and do so, using the same email address and password that you used to sign up for Heroku.

Next we'll need to add our SSH keys. Unlike Bitbucket or Github though, we don't have to copy and paste them into the website; we can do it from the terminal:

```
1  $ heroku keys:add
2
```

Heroku will find your SSH key itself.

Finally, we need to create an actual app on Heroku:

```
1  $ heroku create
2
```

Heroku will output a bunch of text on the terminal screen. Take a look, see that URL? That's the URL of our new App. Sure, we haven't pushed our code up to Heroku yet, but when we do, that's where it will sit:

https://intense-caverns-8282.herokuapp.com

It probably looks like a fairly strange URL (they seem to autogenerate them). You can change the URL to something easier to remember. All we have to do is enter a simple command into the terminal.

```
1  $ heroku rename (pick a name like pinterested12)
2
```

So if you wanted to name your app pinterested 12, you would type in

```
1  $ heroku remane pinterested12
2
```

I'd suggest you name it pinterested, but the name has to be unique and pinterested has already been taken.

I renamed my app, the URL is now:

https://pinterested99.herokuapp.com

Yours will be whatever you changed your app to.

With Heroku, it's easy to use a custom domain name too; like www.pinterested99.com and I'll show you how to do that towards the end of this book. No need to put the cart before the horse, we can use the whatever.herokuapp.com URL while we're building the thing.

PUSHING CODE TO HEROKU

Now that we have Heroku all set up, it's time to push our code up there. Pushing code to Heroku is very similar to pushing code to Bitbucket or Github, in fact we'll use the same three commands – and then just add a fourth for Heroku:

```
1  $ git add .
2  $ git commit –am "add your comment"
3  $ git push
4  $ git push heroku master
5
```

The first three lines are familiar to us already; they just save your changes with git and push up to Bitbucket (or Github if you've chosen to use them). The only difference is the last line: git push heroku master and that simply pushes all your code up to Heroku.

After you run that command, you'll usually have to wait for a minute or two and while you wait you'll see a whole bunch of gobbledigook text outputted to the screen. That's totally normal. Rails is just doing it's thing.

Once it finishes pushing to Heroku, your app is live! You can head over to pinterested99.herokuapp.com (or whatever URL you selected) and see your app live.

Sure, there isn't much there yet. But it'll start to go faster now...

IMPORTANT

Before you push your code to Heroku for the first time, we need to make a quick change to our Gemfile. Our app is currently using a lightweight database called sqlite3 which comes installed with Rails. Heroku no longer allows that database, so we need to change our Gemfile. Open the Gemfile and delete the line:

/Gemfile
```
1  .
2  .
3  gem 'sqlite3'
4  .
5
```

Just go ahead and remove it completely. Next add this bit of code to the bottom of your Gemfile:

/Gemfile

```
1  .
2  .
3   group :development, :test do
4     gem 'sqlite3'
5   end
6
7   group :production do
8     gem 'pg',          '0.17.1'
9     gem 'rails_12factor', '0.0.2'
10  end
11
```

If you take a look at that code, you can sort of see that it's telling our app to use the sqlite3 database on our local development environment (and test environment, but we won't be talking about test stuff in this book), and to use pg and rails_12factor for the production environment (Heroku).

PG stands for Postgres, and that's the production level database we'll be using up on Heroku (rails_12factor is something that goes with it).

After you add those changes to the Gemfile, you need to run the bundle install command in the terminal, but slightly differently than usual:

```
1  $ bundle install --without production
2
```

That '--without production' flag tells Rails to ignore the postgres stuff.

Now you can save your work and push your code to Heroku for the first time:

```
1  $ git add .
2  $ git commit –am "add your comment"
3  $ git push
4  $ git push heroku master
```

MOVING FORWARD – GETTING HELP

We're almost ready to start doing some real stuff. You'll be surprised how quickly our app comes together.

But before we get started, I wanted to talk very briefly about errors.

They say that computer programming is 90% error fixing. Basically, you're going to spend a little bit of time writing computer code (around 10% of your time), and then 90% of your time fixing the screw-ups that you made in that 10% of writing code.

That certainly seems to hold true in Rails. Lots of things can go wrong, and WILL go wrong. There's no shame in asking for help when you get stumped with a problem you can't solve, in fact – it's essential.

As a coder, you're going to have to get good at searching for help over at Google. Luckily, Rails is pretty good about giving you a heads up about errors. You can usually copy the error summary and then paste it right into Google.

Chances are, someone else had that same problem and has written down how to solve it; either on a message board, or in a blog post, or some other way.
More often than not, when you search for help at Google, you'll come across an answer posted on a website called **StackOverflow.com**

StackOverflow.com is basically a social network for coders...not just Rails coders, but ALL coders. People go there to ask questions, and answer other people's questions.

It's a real community and I highly suggest you go check it out, sign up for a free account, and scope out the lay of the land because you will definitely need the support of your fellow coders along the way.

As for this book in particular, I highly recommend you sign up for the "Learning Ruby on Rails For Web Development" course at Codemy.com

(http://Codemy.com/rails)

Not only do I walk you through every section of this book in video form, but I'm also available to answer any questions you have along the way. Just post them below any video where you get stuck, and I'll usually respond within an hour or two (I'm there all the time).

The price for one course is usually $97 but I'll knock off $22 as a thank-you for reading this book, just use coupon code **amazon** when you check out.

The price is kind of a joke when you compare it to the hundreds or thousands of dollars that most online Rails courses charge, but I'm weird like that. I'm less interested in making money and more interested in making sure you learn how to use Rails...otherwise I'd charge $899 for the course!

Either way, get used to asking for help – everyone does (me included!).

CHAPTER TWO

BUILDING OUT OUR SAMPLE APP

So we've got our development environment all set up, we've got version control up and running and we're ready to deploy our app to Heroku whenever we like. It's time to start building out our app!

In this chapter we're going to start building out pages for our app. In the next chapter we'll begin to style the app using Bootstrap, which is a CSS framework that's amazingly easy to use and allows you to build very good looking web sites without any real frontend design experience.

Before we get into Bootstrap though, let's go ahead and add another page to our app. Up until now we just have our Index page, but any app you ever build will probably have more than one page; so how do we create more pages?

ADDING MORE PAGES TO THE APP

So let's add an "About Us" page. Most websites have an "About Us" page. Adding a page is fairly easy; in fact it just takes three simple steps.

1. Manually create a page file in our Views directory.

2. Add the page to our Controller (we haven't really looked at the controller yet).

3. Set the page's Route in /config/routes.rb

Step one is easy, we just need to manually create a page in our Views directory. Generally speaking, we want to add the page to the same directory (folder) where our Index page is sitting, though that isn't absolutely necessary. In our case, that directory is /app/views/home/

To add a new page, just right click on the /app/views/home directory on the left-hand side of your development environment, and choose "New File".

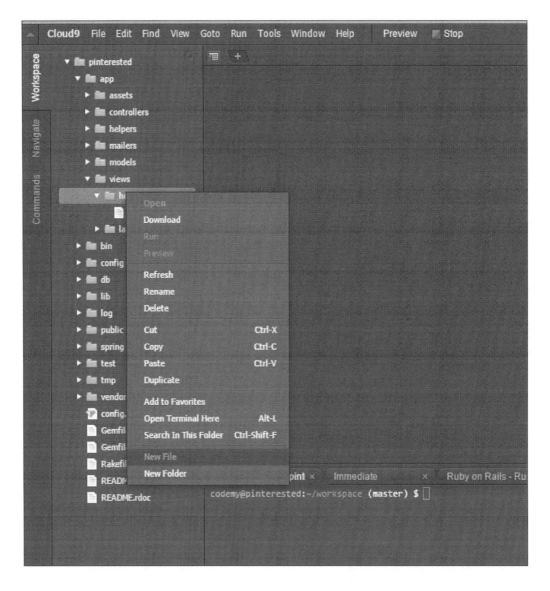

(Create New File – Right Click on /app/views/home/ select "New File")

A new file will appear in front of your eyes, right there in the /app/views/home directory, and you'll need to name it. Let's call it about.html.erb

Remember, most web pages tend to end in .html but we end ours in .html.erb so that we can use embedded Ruby on the page (and we'll see an example of that soon).

So now our about.html.erb page exists, but there's nothing in there; so double click it pull it up in the editor.

You might want to double click the index.html.erb file that's sitting in the same directory too, just to jolt your memory as to what it looks like. Right now we've only got a couple of lines in our index.html.erb file:

```
1  <h1>Welcome To My App</h1>
2  <p>It's Gonna Kick All Ass...</p>
3
```

And that's fine for now...but let's get back to our about.html.erb file. Open it in the editor (it should be empty) and add a couple lines:

```
1  <h1>About Me...</h1>
2  <p>My Name Is (YOUR NAME HERE) and I'm Building a Pinterest Clone</p>
3
```

Type that in and then hit Control and S (Ctrl + S) to save the file; Command S on a Mac.

So now that file exists, but our app doesn't really know it yet...so that brings us to step two: Add the page to our Controller.

ADD OUR NEW PAGE TO THE CONTROLLER

We haven't really looked at our Controller yet, but let's do so now:

/app/controllers/home_controller.rb
```
1   class HomeController < ApplicationController
2     def index
3     end
4   end
5
```

So there really isn't much in there. This is our home controller. Why home? Because when we first generated our index page with the command: "$ rails generate controller home index", that command created a home controller (you can see it right there in the command).

Basically our controller right now isn't doing much of anything except defining that the index page exists. So let's modify it to let it know about our new About page. Easy enough:

/app/controllers/home_controller.rb
```
1   class HomeController < ApplicationController
2     def index
3     end
4
5     def about
6     end
4
5   end
6
```

We've just added two little lines, *def about* and *end*. That's all we need to do there. Now we can move on to the third and final step, adding a route to our new page.

SET THE ROUTE FOR OUR NEW PAGE

We've fiddled with our routes.rb file earlier when we changed the route to our index.html.erb file to make it our root route. Now we just need to add a route for our new about page:

/config/routes.rb
```
1  Rails.application.routes.draw do
2  root 'home#index'
3  get 'home/about'
4  .
5  .
6  end
7
```

Basically we just added the line: get 'home/about', the rest is how we left it from earlier when we added our index root route.

Be sure to save the file with Control and S (Ctrl + S) or Command S on a Mac (I can stop telling you to save files now, right? Every time we make a change to a file, just assume that you need to save it and hit Ctrl + S).

That's all there is to it, we've now successfully added an About Us Page. Fire up your web browser and point it to /home/about to see for yourself:

https://pinterested-codemy.c9.io/home/about (or whatever your URL is)

That wasn't too terribly hard, was it? That's how to add a page to your app manually, after the fact.

You can also generate pages automatically at the very start of building your app when you created the Index page by simply passing the names of the pages you want to create on to your 'generate' command.

Remember, our generate command to create our index page was:

```
1  $ rails generate controller home index
2
```

That command generated the index page and the home controller. But you could have created an about page (and any other pages you wish) at the same time like this:

```
1  $ rails generate controller home index about contact faq
2
```

You'll notice that command is the same as the one we used to create our index page; I just tacked on a few more page names to the end (about contact and faq).

That command will do everything for you. It'll create the pages themselves (about.html.erb, contact.html.erb, and faq.html.erb) inside your /app/views/home/ directory.

It will also add each of those pages to your /app/controllers/home_controller.rb Controller (Step two), and even create routes to each of those pages in your Routes file, /config/routes.rb (Step Three).

You don't really want to use that command more than once. So if you started your app by using this command: $ rails generate controller home index and then later wanted to add more pages, you should add them manually like I showed you how to do at the beginning of this chapter, don't try to run the generate command again and tack on the pages that way. It might work, but things can get weird.

ADDING LINKS TO WEB PAGES

So now that we have two pages (index and about) we should probably link them together so that people can navigate between them.

Rails handles hyperlinks a little bit differently than regular HTML. With regular HTML a link looks like this:

```
1   <a href="about.html">About Us</a>
2
```

You can still create links that way if you want, but Rails has a better way using embedded ruby. That same link will look like this with embedded Ruby:

```
1   <%= link_to 'About Us', home_about_path %>
2
```

So let's take a look at that line of code because there are several things going on here that we need to talk about.

First of all, notice how the tag starts and ends:

```
1   <%=  ...  %>
2
```

Those are the opening tags and closing tags for embedded Ruby. All embedded Ruby tags will look like that (for the most part, the exception is that some leave off the = sign but we'll talk about that later).

Next, *link_to* is how Ruby tells our app we want to make a hyperlink, and the 'About Us' is the anchor text that will show up on the web page. Pretty straight forward.

The only tricky part of this whole thing is the ***home_about_path*** bit. That needs some explaining!

Basically we're just telling our app what route to follow. Remember when we created our 'About' page and added the route:

/config/routes.rb

```
1  Rails.application.routes.draw do
2  root 'home#index'
3  get 'home/about'
4  .
5  .
6  end
7
```

get 'home/about' is telling our app that the route to our about page is home/about and that's what we're telling our link to point towards. Instead of writing it as home/about for the link, the convention is to user home_about_path.

The _path at the end is saying "hey, it's the path to home_about".

Make sense?

So how will we know what routes are available for links? It's easy to sort of eyeball our */config/routes.rb* file right now and see; but that's because we've only got two pages. As our app becomes more complicated, we'll be adding many more pages and things can get a little hard to just eyeball.

Luckily there's a command you can enter into the terminal that will show you all the routes:

```
1  $ rake routes
2
```

The rake routes command will show you all the routes currently available to you, as well as how they should be formatted for the link_to tag. Let's run the command again and look at the output:

```
1  $ rake routes
2  Prefix Verb     URI Pattern                 Controller#Action
3    root          GET  /                       home#index
4    home_about    GET  /home/about(.:format)   home#about
5
```

The first column shows the route you need to use for the link_to tag (you just need to slap a _path to the end of it). Notice the home_about path.

But wait, shouldn't the index path be home_index_path? No! You'll notice when we ran the rake routes command, it lists our Index page's route as root. That means if we wanted to link to that page using a link_to tag, it would look like this:

```
1  <%= link_to 'Home', root_path %>
2
```

Make sense?

So let's add our two links to our two pages, first let's add them to our Index page:

/app/views/home/index.html.erb
```
1  <%= link_to 'Home', root_path %>
2  <%= link_to 'About Us', home_about_path %>
3  <h1>Welcome To My App</h1>
4  <p>It's Gonna Kick All Ass...</p>
5
```

Save and close. Now let's add them to our About Us Page:

/app/views/home/about.html.erb
```
1  <%= link_to 'Home', root_path %>
2  <%= link_to 'About Us', home_about_path %>
3  <h1>About Me...</h1>
4  <p>My Name Is (YOUR NAME HERE) and I'm Building a Pinterest Clone</p>
5
```

Save, and then head over to your web browser and reload your page:

https://pinterested-codemy.c9.io (or whatever your URL is).

You should see those two links right at the top of the page. You can click on the 'About Us' link and it should go to your about page, where you can click on the 'Home' link and return home.

Now we're getting somewhere! It's not much functionality, but it IS functionality and we can build on it!

ADDING LINKS TO EACH PAGE IS TOO MUCH WORK

So we just added links to each of our web pages, but that was too much work because we had to add them to each of our pages. Sure, we only have two pages (index and about) but normally you'd have many more...sometimes hundreds or even thousands more. You wouldn't want to edit each of those pages every time you wanted to update a link, would you? Of course not.

Luckily Ruby gives us a solution called a 'Partial'.

CREATING PARTIALS

A partial is basically an include file. It lets us include the contents of one file in another. Creating partials is a two-step process.

1. First create your partial file
2. Next call the partial file from another file

Creating a partial file is done in a similar way to creating our 'About' page (but we don't need to add a route or fiddle with the Controller). Just right click on your /app/views/home/ folder and select "New File". There is one small difference.

When you **name** your new file, put an **underscore** in front of it. So if you wanted to create a partial file called header.html.erb you would name that

_header.html.erb

In fact, do that now. Right click on your /app/views/home/ directory folder and create a new file called _header.html.erb

Now double click that file to open it in the text editor, and let's copy in our two links:

/app/views/home/_header.html.erb
```
1  <%= link_to 'Home', root_path %>
2  <%= link_to 'About Us', home_about_path %>
3
```

Save that file and close it. That's all there is to step one of creating a partial. Let's move on to step two. To call a partial in another file, you'll use this embedded Ruby tag:

```
1  <%= render 'home/header' %>
2
```

It's pretty straight forward. Render tells our app to render the partial, and 'home/header' tells our app where to find the partial file.

You might think that it should instead be 'home/_header.html.erb' instead of the simpler 'home/header', but it's not. Rails knows that by calling render home/header you're really asking it to display your _header.html.erb file.

So let's change our Index page to reflect this and get rid of the links we put in earlier:

/app/views/home/index.html.erb

```
1  <%= render 'home/header' %>
2  <h1>Welcome To My App</h1>
3  <p>It's Gonna Kick All Ass...</p>
4
```

Save that file, then head back to your web browser and reload the page at:

https://pinterested-codemy.c9.io (or whatever your URL is)

It should look the same as it did earlier, with the two links to Home and About Us at the top of the page. The only difference is that those links were called from our Header partial.

You might think it wise to replace the links on your About Us Page with the <%= render 'home/header' %> tag, BUT WAIT!

Before you do that, Rails makes this all EVEN EASIER...which means that it's now time to discuss the application.html.erb file.

INTRODUCING LAYOUTS/APPLICATION.HTML.ERB

You might have noticed a **Layouts** folder in your /app/views/ folder. What is it? The Layouts folder contains a file called application.html.erb and that's a special file.

It holds the skeleton framework for every web page in our app. Let's take a look at it:

/app/views/layouts/application.html.erb

```
1   <!DOCTYPE html>
2   <html>
3   <head>
4     <title>Workspace</title>
5     <%= stylesheet_link_tag   'application', media: 'all', 'data-turbolinks-track' => true %>
6     <%= javascript_include_tag 'application', 'data-turbolinks-track' => true %>
7     <%= csrf_meta_tags %>
8   </head>
9   <body>
10
11  <%= yield %>
12
13  </body>
14  </html>
15
```

So what's going on here? Basically the contents of this file get called and outputted to the web browser any time a page of your site gets viewed online. The interesting line to notice here is the **<%= yield %>** tag.

Basically, that tag is calling the contents of your page and outputting it right there.

So if you went to: **https://pinterested-codemy.c9.io/home/about**

The application.html.erb file gets called behind the scenes, it grabs all the stuff from your about.html.erb file and outputs it where the <%= yield %> tag is.

In fact, if you go to your **https://pinterested-codemy.c9.io/home/about** page in your web browser and view the page source (right click on the screen and choose "view page source"), you'll see code that looks just like the application.html.erb file.

```
     view-source:https://pinterested-codemy.c9.io/home/about
 1  <!DOCTYPE html>
 2  <html>
 3  <head>
 4    <title>Workspace</title>
 5    <link data-turbolinks-track="true" href="/assets/home.css?body=1" media="all" rel="stylesheet" />
 6  <link data-turbolinks-track="true" href="/assets/application.css?body=1" media="all" rel="stylesheet" />
 7    <script data-turbolinks-track="true" src="/assets/jquery.js?body=1"></script>
 8  <script data-turbolinks-track="true" src="/assets/jquery_ujs.js?body=1"></script>
 9  <script data-turbolinks-track="true" src="/assets/turbolinks.js?body=1"></script>
10  <script data-turbolinks-track="true" src="/assets/home.js?body=1"></script>
11  <script data-turbolinks-track="true" src="/assets/application.js?body=1"></script>
12    <meta content="authenticity_token" name="csrf-param" />
13  <meta content="TyCZ1C98dp/l+dcnZUqRJksi11ARoxEaDRBNf6QwHO0=" name="csrf-token" />
14  </head>
15  <body>
16
17  <a href="/">Home</a>
18  <a href="/home/about">About Us</a>
19
20  <h1>About Us</h1>
21  <p>My name is John Elder and I'm building a Pinterest Clone at Codemy.com</p>
22
23  </body>
24  </html>
25
```

(https://pinterested-codemy.c9.io/home/about View Source - Source Code)

Pretty neat.

What that means for us, is there's no need to render our Header partial on every page of our site, we can simply render it on our application.html.erb file right above the <%= yield %> tag!

So let's do that now. Open your index.html.erb file and erase the partial line:

```
1  <%= render 'home/header' %>
2
```

Just take it right out, and save the index.html.erb file. Now we're going to add that exact line to our application.html.erb file:

/app/views/layouts/application.html.erb

```
1   <!DOCTYPE html>
2   <html>
3   <head>
4     <title>Workspace</title>
5     <%= stylesheet_link_tag   'application', media: 'all', 'data-turbolinks-track' => true %>
6     <%= javascript_include_tag 'application', 'data-turbolinks-track' => true %>
7     <%= csrf_meta_tags %>
8   </head>
9   <body>
10  <%= render 'home/header' %>
11  <%= yield %>
12
13  </body>
14  </html>
15
```

See how we added it to line 10? Save the file and close, now head back to your site: **https://pinterested-codemy.c9.io** (or whatever your URL is)

You should see our Header links from our Header partial there at the top of the screen, and if you click the About Us link, you should see the Header links at the top of it too!

Now any page we create in our app will have those links at the top of the screen. And any time we want to change the links in the top Header, all we have to do is edit the list of links in our _header.html.erb file one time and the change will be reflected on all of our pages.

Pretty cool.

CHAPTER THREE

ADDING BOOTSTRAP

So our app is starting to come together. We've got a couple of pages, and the beginning of a header navigation system. It's time to start styling our app to make it look a little more professional.

To do that, we're going to use something called "Bootstrap", which is a CSS framework that was created by a couple of guys at Twitter. It used to be called Twitter Bootstrap, but the guys have since left Twitter and taken Bootstrap with them, and now maintain it full-time on their own.

Bootstrap is one of the most popular CSS frameworks out there because it is incredibly easy to use and you don't need any front-end design experience to use it.

Take a minute to go check it out at: **GetBootstrap.com**

Click on the "Components" link at the top of the page and just sort of scroll through all the stuff on that page. You'll see a lot of the different things you can add to your website listed there.

Below each item you'll see a little snippet of code. Adding the item to your page is as easy as copying and pasting that code onto your site (in most cases).

INSTALLING BOOTSTRAP

To use Bootstrap in our App we need to add the Bootstrap Gem. The name of the Gem is "bootstrap-sass ", so let's head over to RubyGems.org and check it out (you always want to get into the habit of going to RubyGems.org and checking out a Gem before blindly installing it.

At RubyGems.org search for bootstrap-sass and it should be the first one listed:

bootstrap-sass 3.3.1.0
Twitter's Bootstrap, converted to Sass and ready to drop into Rails or Compass

**Note: the version number 3.3.1.0 might be different by the time this book is published, it's no big deal – they're always updating Gems.

Go ahead and click on it and you should see this standard page:

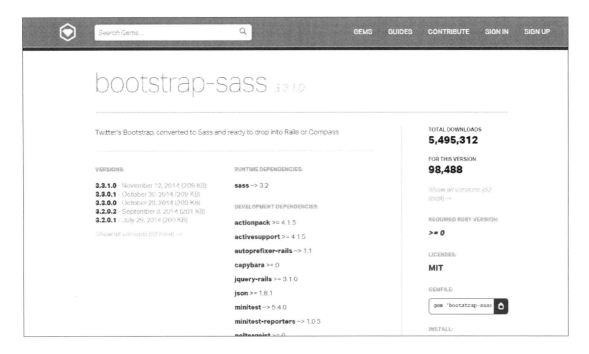

(RubyGems.org bootstrap-sass page)

There on the right-hand side of the screen you should see a little box labelled "GEMFILE:" with a little clipboard icon under it. Click the clipboard icon to copy the Gem reference and version number; it should look like this:

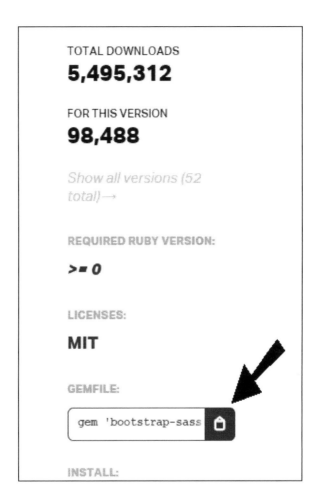

(gem 'bootstrap-sass', '~> 3.3.1.0')

Under that you should also see a link to the Gem's Documentation. That's where you would normally get instructions for installing and using the Gem. Take a minute to check it out and read through it.

So let's go ahead and add Bootstrap to our app. We need to add the reference to the bootstrap-sass Gem to our Gemfile:

/Gemfile

```
1    source 'https://rubygems.org'
2    gem 'rails', '4.1.6'
3    gem 'sass-rails', '~> 4.0.3'
4    gem 'uglifier', '>= 1.3.0'
5    gem 'coffee-rails', '~> 4.0.0'
6    gem 'jquery-rails'
7    gem 'turbolinks'
8    gem 'jbuilder', '~> 2.0'
9  gem 'sdoc', '~> 0.4.0',        group: :doc
10 gem 'spring',      group: :development
11 gem 'bootstrap-sass', '~> 3.3.1.0'
12
13   group :development, :test do
14     gem 'sqlite3'
15   end
16
17   group :production do
18     gem 'pg',          '0.17.1'
19     gem 'rails_12factor', '0.0.2'
20   end
21
```

Notice line 11 is what we added. Save the file and close it, now we need to run the bundle install command like always when adding a new Gem.

```
1  $ bundle install
2
```

Sometimes those two steps are enough to install a Gem, but not this time. We need to do a few more things (as per the instructions in the Documentation at RubyGems.org).

Bootstrap is a CSS framework, so we need to add a CSS file to our app. You can name it just about anything, so I'm going to name it bootstraply.css.scss and it goes here: /app/assets/stylesheets/bootstraply.css.scss

We haven't really talked about the /app/assets/ folders yet, but if you just glance at it you'll see that it contains three directories (images, javascripts, and stylesheets). We won't get into it now, but you can guess that this is where your images, javascripts and stylesheets go...

For now, just right-click on the stylesheets directory and select "New File" (like we've done in the past) and name the new file bootstraply.css.scss

Next, open that newly created bootstraply.css.scss file and add these two lines of code:

```
1
2  @import "bootstrap-sprockets";
3  @import "bootstrap";
4
```

Actually, leave a couple of spaces above those two lines because we'll be adding more stuff to the top of that file later on.

We're almost finished, now we just need to add a reference to some javascript stuff that Bootstrap uses. Add these lines to our Javascript reference file:

/app/assets/javascripts/application.js

1 //= require jquery

2 .

3 .

4 //= require bootstrap-sprockets

5 //= require bootstrap

6 //= require_tree .

7

There will already be a bunch of stuff in that file, just put the two lines in bold above the //=require_tree . line and you should be good to go.

That should do it! It's a good idea to stop and restart your server whenever you add a new Gem, so let's do that now. Next head back to your website and reload the page: **https://pinterested-codemy.c9.io** (or whatever your URL is)

Home About Us

Welcome To My App

It's Gonna Kick All Ass...

(https://pinterested-codemy.c9.io with Bootstrap Installed)

Notice anything different? Your page should look *slightly* different. The link colors should be different and the font should look a little different. That's Bootstrap at work.

You'll also notice that all the text is crunched up against the very side of the screen. Let's fix that real quick. All we need to do is open our application.html.erb file and wrap the <%= yield %> tag in a container div:

/app/views/layouts/application.html.erb

```
1   <!DOCTYPE html>
2   <html>
3   <head>
4     <title>Workspace</title>
5     <%= stylesheet_link_tag   'application', media: 'all', 'data-turbolinks-track' => true %>
6     <%= javascript_include_tag 'application', 'data-turbolinks-track' => true %>
7     <%= csrf_meta_tags %>
8   </head>
9   <body>
10    <%= render 'home/header' %>
11
12  <div class="container">
13    <%= yield %>
14  </div>
15
16  </body>
17  </html>
15
```

(https://pinterested-codemy.c9.io With Container Class Gutter)

That should add a gutter on the left and right side of the screen. I tend to do this with all my websites because it looks good and it's a standard layout thing to do.

PLAYING WITH BOOTSTRAP

So let's play around with Bootstrap a little bit. Let's start out by adding a Jumbotron to our Index page. Head over to GetBootStrap.com and click the "Components" tab at the top of the screen. Next, scroll down the list of links on the right hand side of the screen till you see the "Jumbotron" link, click it.

You'll see a Jumbotron with a bit of code below it:

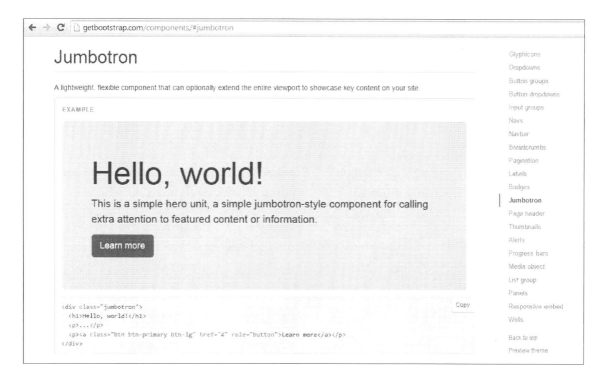

(GetBootstrap.com Jumbotron Component)

Take a look at the code below it. You'll notice that to add a Jumbotron to our site, we just need to wrap whatever we want the Jumbotron to include with this tag:

```
1  <div class="jumbotron">
2  .
3  .
4  </div>
```

So let's do that right now to our Index page:

/app/views/home/index.html.erb

```
1  <div class="jumbotron">
2    <h1>Welcome To My App</h1>
3    <p>It's Gonna Kick All Ass...</p>
4  </div>
5
```

Save it, then take a look at the page in your web browser. Pretty neat!

Now let's see how to make some buttons with Bootstrap. Let's add two buttons to our Jumbotron. Buttons are not listed on the "Components" page at GetBootstrap.com, but rather on the "CSS" page, so click the "CSS" link at the top of the page. Then, click the "Buttons" link on the right hand menu. Scroll down till you see the "Options" section for the buttons.

(http://getbootstrap.com/css/#buttons)

You see we have six different color options (white, blue, green, light blue, orange, and red). The corresponding code for each button can be found below the button images:

```
1  <button type="button" class="btn btn-default">Default</button>
2
```

Notice the *Class=* part. That's where you designate the color type. Default is white, Primary is blue, Success is green, Info is light blue, Warning is orange, and Danger is red.

Normally we only need to copy and paste the code from GetBootstrap.com into our app (like we did with the Jumbotron), but buttons are a little different because they are links, and we learned earlier that Rails does links a little differently (remember we used embedded Ruby to generate our page links).

We'll need to use the same embedded Ruby, but with a little twist. I'll show you how by adding two buttons to our Index page inside the jumbotron:

/app/views/home/index.html.erb
```
1  <div class="jumbotron">
2    <h1>Welcome To My App</h1>
3    <p>It's Gonna Kick All Ass...</p>
4    <%= link_to 'About Us', home_about_path, class: 'btn btn-default' %>
5    <%= link_to 'Home', root_path, class: 'btn btn-primary' %>
6  </div>
7
```

(https://pinterested-codemy.c9.io with Jumbotron and Buttons)

The link_to tag is exactly the same as we've used before, except we added a comma at the end and the *class: 'btn btn-default'* bit at the end. That tells Rails that this isn't just a link, but it's a button link. And I got that class stuff directly from the code beneath the buttons there at GetBootstrap.com

You'll notice I added two different colored buttons, a white one and a blue one just to mix things up. You can also change the size as well (see size listings in the button section at Getbootstrap.com).

For instance, if we had wanted to make one of the buttons large, it would look like this:

```
1  <%= link_to 'About Us', home_about_path, class: 'btn btn-default btn-lg' %>
2
```

**Note: I should point out that I use single quotes (') in the link_to tag above, but you can also use regular double quotes (") if you prefer. Rails accepts either.

ADDING A NAVBAR

So we've played around with Bootstrap a bit; adding a Jumbotron and some buttons, but now it's time to pull out the big guns and add a Navbar.

(http://getbootstrap.com/components/#navbar Bootstrap Navbar)

Navbars are located on the "Components" page at GetBootstrap.com, so go check them out. We'll use the first one they have listed, but I don't want a search bar or links right by the "Brand" logo, so I'll simply erase those lines from the code listed below the Navbar example.

We'll also replace the default links with the links to our exact pages. Where should we put all this code? Surely not at the top of every page of our site! Nope, we'll put it just once in our _header.html.erb partial file that gets called and outputted on every page automatically. In fact, we can erase what's in that file now and put our Navbar code:

/app/views/home/_header.html.erb

```
1   <nav class="navbar navbar-default" role="navigation">
2    <div class="container">
3     <!-- Brand and toggle get grouped for better mobile display -->
4     <div class="navbar-header">
5                    <button type="button" class="navbar-toggle collapsed" data-
6     toggle="collapse" data-target="#bs-example-navbar-collapse-1">
7       <span class="sr-only">Toggle navigation</span>
8       <span class="icon-bar"></span>
9       <span class="icon-bar"></span>
10      <span class="icon-bar"></span>
11     </button>
12     <a class="navbar-brand" href="#">Brand</a>
13     </div>
14
15     <!-- Collect the nav links, forms, and other content for toggling -->
16     <div class="collapse navbar-collapse" id="bs-example-navbar-collapse-1">
17        <ul class="nav navbar-nav navbar-right">
18          <li><%= link_to 'Home', root_path %></li>
19          <li><%= link_to 'About Me', home_about_path %></li>
20        </ul>
21     </div><!-- /.navbar-collapse -->
22    </div><!-- /.container-fluid -->
23   </nav>
24
```

There's only a few differences between the code above and the code snippet listed at GetBootstrap.com

First, notice on line 2: <div class="container">, the default listed at GetBootstrap is <div class="container-fluid"> but I took out the fluid tag because I don't want it to be fluid.

Next, notice line 18 and 19, that's where our links go. The only difference between those two links and our old two links is that these two are wrapped in <li> and </li> tags, which is necessary for the Navbar.

Finally, I took out the reference to the search form and the default dropdown links that come with it because I don't want dropdown links.

So go ahead and save that file and hit reload at your site and your page should now look like this:

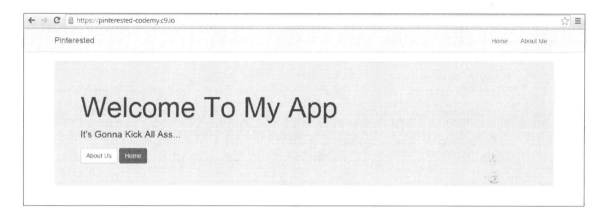

(https://pinterested-codemy.c9.io/ With Navbar and Jumbotron and Buttons)

You can also change line 12 above to say "Pinterested" instead of brand. In fact, let's change that line and make it an embedded Ruby link instead of a normal HTML link. Notice the HTML link has a class of "navbar-brand", we'll have to slap that onto the end of our Ruby link just like we did for the buttons.

```
1  <%= link_to 'Pinterested', root_path, class: 'navbar-brand' %>
2
```

Now our Navbar will say Pinterested instead of Brand and have a working link.

Throughout the rest of this book we'll do more stuff with Bootstrap, but I think you can probably already see how easy it is to work with and how quickly you can throw up some really professional looking front-end design stuff to make your site look really good.

Take some time to play around with Bootstrap on your own. Look through the different thing it offers and try some of them out. Have some fun with it and we'll get back into the serious stuff in the next chapter.

CUSTOMIZING BOOTSTRAP

Right out of the box, Bootstrap gives you a lot of flexibility, but you can actually customize Bootstrap to make it look exactly how you want it to look, and it's fairly easy. Don't like the color of the Navbar? We can change that. Don't like the color of the Jumbotron or buttons? We can change that too.

Bootstrap is built on something called LESS which is a dynamic stylesheet language that allows you to define variable and do different things.

HOWEVER, our version of Bootstrap doesn't use LESS, it uses SASS (remember when we installed the Bootstrap Gem, it was called bootstrap-sass?

SASS stands for "Syntactically Awesome StyleSheets" and is a scripting language similar to LESS.

Don't worry, you don't need to know much about SASS or LESS, all you need to know is one thing...LESS uses @ signs and SASS uses $ signs. We won't get much deeper than that!

So what?

SASS allows us to customize Bootstrap down to the nth level and get it to look *exactly* how we want it to look. To see how, head back to GetBootstrap.com and click the "Customize" link at the top of the screen. Next click the "Less Variables" link on the right-hand side of the screen.

You should see a big list of things, all of which can be customized.

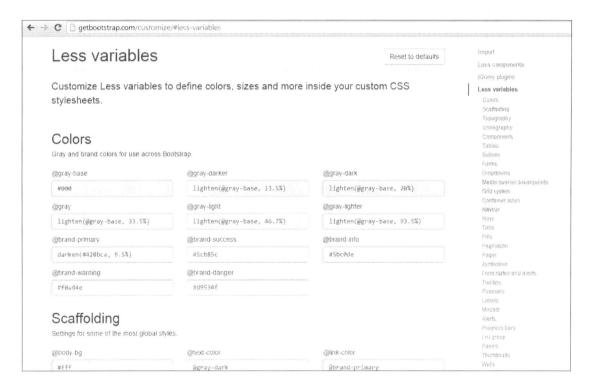

(http://getbootstrap.com/customize/#less-variables – Available Variables To Customize)

Browse through the list and pick something out. Let's look at the Jumbotron variables since we've got a Jumbotron on our Index page.

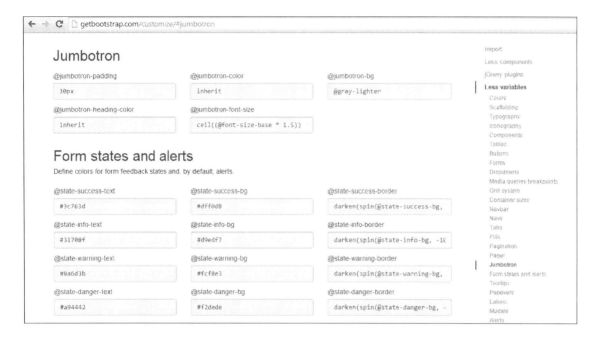

(http://getbootstrap.com/customize/#jumbotron)

All of the things listed here are things we can customize for our app. For instance, let's take this one:

```
1  @jumbotron-bg
2
```

Notice the @ sign? That's because it's Less. But like I said, we aren't using Less, we're using Sass so we need to change the @ to a $ when we use these things.

And how do we use them? We simply add them to our bootstraply.css.scss file that we created earlier when we installed the Bootstrap Gem.

/app/assets/stylesheets/bootstraply.css.scss

```
1  $jumbotron-bg: blue;
2  .
3  .
4  @import "bootstrap-sprockets";
5  @import "bootstrap";
6
7
```

Remember earlier when I told you to add some space above those two @import lines we added when we first created this file? That's because any time you add a Sass variable to this file, it needs to be **ABOVE** those two lines.

So what did we do here? We told our Bootstrap to make the background of our Jumbotron blue. Notice the format; $variable: output;

You have your Sass variable (that we took from the "Customize" page at GetBootstrap.com) with a dollar sign $ in front of it and a colon behind it, then a space, then whatever output you want (in our case blue) followed by a semi-colon.

I typed blue, just to make a clear example, but normally you would use a color hex code like: #0041a0; which is a shade of blue. So that line would look like this:

```
1  $jumbotron-bg: #0041a0;
2
```

You get the idea. So go ahead and save that and then go check it out by reloading your website at: **https://pinterested-codemy.c9.io** (or whatever your URL is)

The Jumbotron should be blue now. Neat!

And you can do that for any variable in the Less Variables list there on the "Customize" page at GetBootstrap.com

For instance, if you wanted to make the background color of the Navbar green, and the body of the entire site Pink, you would do this:

/app/assets/stylesheets/bootstraply.css.scss

```
1  $jumbotron-bg: blue;
2  $ navbar-default-bg: #014421;
3  $body-bg: #fa9fb9;
4  .
5  .
6  @import "bootstrap-sprockets";
7  @import "bootstrap";
8
```

In fact, try that out and see how it looks! The important thing is that you can customize almost everything, from sizes, to colors, and more.

Spend some time going through that list and looking at all the different things you can customize in Bootstrap. And it's all as easy as adding a single line of code to your bootstrap.css.scss file.

CHAPTER FOUR

ADDING USERS WITH DEVISE

Our app is starting to come together! Now that we've introduced Bootstrap, we can begin to shape the look and feel of the app. But when you get right down to it...our app still doesn't really *do* anything.

It's time to change that.

One of the key components of our app is the ability for people to sign up for a user account, log in, log out, and update their user profile.

We don't want just anyone to be able to post Pinterest-style 'pins' to our site, we want them to sign up and sign in first.

Back in the old days, to write the code needed to handle all of that would be a huge pain in the ass and take a long time. There would have been lots of database work to deal with, and I hate database work!

Luckily, this is Ruby on Rails, and there's a Gem that will handle all of that nasty stuff for us...it's called "Devise".

Devise is a user authentication Gem that will easily handle signing in new users, allowing them to log in, log out, and update their own user profiles. It will also generate all the fill-out forms needed to accomplish this task, and handle all the nasty database stuff too.

All we have to do is install it and configure it, and we're off and running.

Head over to RubyGems.org and search for Devise. As of the writing of this book, Devise has been downloaded and installed nearly ten million times...so yeah, it's a popular Gem (and why not – try to think of any website in the world that doesn't need to sign up, in, and out users!).

As of the writing of this book, devise is on version 3.4.1 so that's what I'll add to our Gemfile:

/Gemfile
```
1    source 'https://rubygems.org'
2
3    gem 'rails', '4.1.6'
4    gem 'sqlite3'
5    gem 'sass-rails', '~> 4.0.3'
6    gem 'uglifier', '>= 1.3.0'
7    gem 'coffee-rails', '~> 4.0.0'
8    gem 'jquery-rails'
9    gem 'turbolinks'
10    gem 'jbuilder', '~> 2.0'
11   gem 'sdoc', '~> 0.4.0',       group: :doc
12   gem 'spring',      group: :development
13   gem 'bootstrap-sass', '~> 3.3.1.0'
14   gem 'devise', '~> 3.4.1'
15
16    group :development, :test do
17     gem 'sqlite3'
18    end
19
20    group :production do
21     gem 'pg',           '0.17.1'
22     gem 'rails_12factor', '0.0.2'
23    end
24
```

As always, when we add a new Gem to our Gemfile, we need to run bundle install:

```
1  $ bundle install
2
```

Of course, Devise does a heck of a lot, and so it shouldn't surprise us that there are more steps to install and configure it than other Gems. You can read those steps in the Devise Documentation found at RubyGems.org but I'm going to walk you through them right now.

First we need to run the generator:

```
1  $ rails generate devise:install
2
```

That will generate a bunch of text to the terminal screen, and if you take a look at that text, you'll notice that it contains instructions for 5 more steps that you need to complete in order to install devise. Don't worry, they aren't too bad and we're going to walk through them right now.

Here are the instructions, straight from Devise's terminal output:

1. Ensure you have defined default url options in your environments files. Here is an example of default_url_options appropriate for a development environment in config/environments/development.rb:

config.action_mailer.default_url_options = { host: 'localhost', port: 3000 }

In production, :host should be set to the actual host of your application.

2. Ensure you have defined root_url to *something* in your config/routes.rb. For example: root to: "home#index"

3. Ensure you have flash messages in app/views/layouts/application.html.erb. For example:

```
<p class="notice"><%= notice %></p>
<p class="alert"><%= alert %></p>
```

4. If you are deploying on Heroku with Rails 3.2 only, you may want to set:

```
config.assets.initialize_on_precompile = false
```

5. You can copy Devise views (for customization) to your app by running:

```
rails g devise:views
```

So let's take a look at these. Right off the bat, we can ignore number four because we aren't using Rails 3.2 – in fact, we're using Rails 4.1.6 or higher.

We can also ignore number two because we've already defined our app's root index page earlier.

So that leaves us with 1, 3, and 5. Let's walk through those now.

STEP ONE

Let's look at step one. Basically we need to add a line of code to two files.

/config/environments/development.rb:

1 .
2 .
3 config.action_mailer.default_url_options = { host: 'localhost', port: 3000 }
4 end
5

Just paste line three at the bottom of that file (above the final 'end' that's already listed there).

Next we need to make a similar change to this file:

/config/environments/production.rb:

1 .
2 .
3 config.action_mailer.default_url_options = { host: ' pinterested99.herokuapp.com' }
4 end
5

Check out line three of this one. It's basically the same as line three from the last file, but instead of **host: 'localhost', port: 3000** we put the URL of out actual live app on Heroku. You should put the URL of whatever you named your app at Heroku.

What's going on here? Well these two files correspond with our development environment and our production environment settings. We're basically just telling our app to use the Webrick server for our local development environment and use Heroku for our production environment.

STEP THREE

Now let's look at Step Three.

Step three wants us to add a bit of code to handle flash messages. Flash messages are basically little automatic prompts that appear on the web site whenever a user does something.

For instance, when a user signs in, they'll get a flash message at the top of the screen that says something like "You have successfully signed in". When they sign out, they'll get one that says "You have successfully signed out", etc.

Devise handles all of these messages automatically, but we need to add a bit of code to our app to show Devise where on the page we want those messages to appear.

Devise has given us some suggested code to post on our site:

```
1  <p class="notice"><%= notice %></p>
2  <p class="alert"><%= alert %></p>
3
```

But we want to change that a bit so that we can use Bootstrap to alter the look and feel of those flash messages. In fact, if you head back to GetBootStrap.com and click the "Components" link, you can scroll through the list and click the "Alerts" link.

A flash message is basically an alert, so we'll be using Bootstrap's alert class. You'll notice Bootstrap offers four colors for alerts; green (success), blue (info), yellow (warning), red (danger). We'll use blue.

So where should we post the code to handle the Devise flash messages? We want those messages to be able to flash on any page of our website, so the logical place to put the code would be our /app/views/layouts/application.html.erb file, right above the <%= yield %> tag and below our container div, so let's do that:

/app/views/layouts/application.html.erb
```
1  .
2  .
3  <div class="container">
4     <% flash.each do |name, msg| %>
5        <%= content_tag(:div, msg, class: "alert alert-info") %>
6     <% end %>
7     <%= yield %>
8  </div>
9  .
10
```

So let's look through this code since it's a little different than what Devise recommended to us.

This is a basic Ruby loop. It's basically saying: "for each flash message, do something", in our case the 'something' is to output the message in a CSS div with class "alert alert-info".

Where did I get class "alert alert-info"? I copied it from the code snippet over at GetBootstrap under the alert for a blue box. So our alerts will be blue.

You'll also notice that the first line Ruby tag doesn't have an equal sign as it's opening tag! <% flash.each do |name, msg| %> (the second line does but not the first).

What gives? Up until now, all of our embedded Ruby has started with a <%= tag. The equal sign means "output this to the screen", and we don't want to output anything when running our loop. We only want to output if the loop becomes true, hence the second line DOES have a <%= tag...because we want to output that stuff.

STEP FIVE

The only thing left to do is add the command from step five into the terminal, so let's go ahead and do that now:

```
1  $ rails g devise:views
2
```

This runs the generator for the devise views. Notice in the past we've always written out generate commands, like this:

```
1  $ rails generate devise:views
2
```

Just typing "g" instead of generate is shorthand and completely acceptable.

After you run this command, check out your /app/views/ directory. You should see a new folder named "devise". That folder contains a bunch of folders and all the new pages that Devise has automatically created to handle stuff like logging in, logging out, editing user profiles, resetting passwords, and stuff like that. Check it out!

The terminal should have displayed a bunch of text too...that's a breakdown of what Devise just added. So you can eyeball it. See all those pages? For instance, let's look at /app/views/devise/registrations/new.html.erb

I'm guessing that's the page that allows people to register for your site (create a 'new' registration). Open it in the text editor and you'll see a "Sign Up" tag right at the top of the file.

How about: app/views/devise/sessions/new.html.erb? That's the page that allows people to log in. When someone logs into your web site they are essentially creating a session. Logging in is the act of creating a new session.

Similarly, logging out is the act of deleting a session.

Devise has created a BUNCH of stuff, and to tell you the truth, we aren't even going to use most of it. So don't get overwhelmed.

We're not *quite* done installing Devise, there's still one more step. We've got devise set up, and we've created our views but we haven't connected Devise with our database so that we can keep track of all those users. Luckily it's not hard, we just need to issue two commands:

```
1  $ rails generate devise user
2  $ rake db:migrate
3
```

WORKING WITH DATABASES IN RAILS

We haven't really talked about databases much, but we need to now. Rails makes working with databases super easy, but you need to understand what's going on.

Whenever you want to do something with databases in Rails, you create a database migration, and then push that migration into the database. Think of a migration as a manifest...a list of stuff you want. Create your list, then stick it in the database.

Just now, when we issued the command: $ rails generate devise user we were creating a migration, and adding 'users' to it. In fact, you can even see the migration file. Migration files are located in the /db/ folder: /db/migrate/

Running that rails generate devise user command created this migration for me: 20141224175632_devise_create_users.rb located here:

/db/migrate/20141224175632_devise_create_users.rb

```
1   class DeviseCreateUsers < ActiveRecord::Migration
2     def change
3       create_table(:users) do |t|
4         ## Database authenticatable
5         t.string :email,          null: false, default: ""
6         t.string :encrypted_password, null: false, default: ""
7
8         ## Recoverable
9         t.string   :reset_password_token
10        t.datetime :reset_password_sent_at
11
12        ## Rememberable
13        t.datetime :remember_created_at
14
15        ## Trackable
16        t.integer  :sign_in_count, default: 0, null: false
17        t.datetime :current_sign_in_at
18        t.datetime :last_sign_in_at
19        t.string   :current_sign_in_ip
20        t.string   :last_sign_in_ip
21
22        ## Confirmable
23        # t.string   :confirmation_token
24        # t.datetime :confirmed_at
25        # t.datetime :confirmation_sent_at
26        # t.string   :unconfirmed_email # Only if using reconfirmable
27
28        ## Lockable
29        # t.integer  :failed_attempts, default: 0, null: false # Only if lock strategy is :failed_attempts
30        # t.string   :unlock_token # Only if unlock strategy is :email or :both
31        # t.datetime :locked_at
```

```
32
33
34      t.timestamps
35    end
36
37    add_index :users, :email,              unique: true
38    add_index :users, :reset_password_token, unique: true
39    # add_index :users, :confirmation_token,  unique: true
40    # add_index :users, :unlock_token,        unique: true
41    end
42  end
43
```

So there's a lot of stuff here, and you don't really need to know what any of it means, but take a look through it and see if anything jumps out at you.

We can see there's a reference to emails and passwords (because our users will log in with emails and passwords), there's some time stuff so we can keep track of when someone is logged in, and there's password reset stuff.

Like I said though, we don't really need to know what any of that stuff means at this point, or really ever. Just know that we've created a migration.

To push that migration into our database, we issued the $ rake db:migrate command.

DEVELOPMENT DATABASE VS. PRODUCTION DATABASE

Before we go any further, we need to talk databases a bit (Since we're using them now). I mentioned this earlier when we set up Heroku for the first time but I wanted to touch on it again.

In our development environment, we're using a database called: sqlite3. It's a very light-weight database that comes installed with Rails. In fact, if you look at your Gemfile, you'll see a reference to it.

Like I mentioned earlier, sqlite3 isn't really an appropriate database to use for our finished production level website. We needed to designate another database for that.

We're going to use the Postgres database. Why? Heroku likes Postgres, and it's super easy to use. The only thing we really need to do is add the Postgres Gem to our Gemfile (which we did earlier). You'll remember it was a little more complicated than adding a regular Gem, simply because we need to tell our app to use sqlite3 for development and postgres for production...but still pretty simple.

So here's what we did:

/Gemfile
```
1   source 'https://rubygems.org'
2
3   gem 'rails', '4.1.6'
4   gem 'sass-rails', '~> 4.0.3'
5   gem 'uglifier', '>= 1.3.0'
6   gem 'coffee-rails', '~> 4.0.0'
7   gem 'jquery-rails'
8   gem 'turbolinks'
9   gem 'jbuilder', '~> 2.0'
10  gem 'sdoc', '~> 0.4.0',        group: :doc
11  gem 'spring',      group: :development
12  gem 'bootstrap-sass', '~> 3.3.1.0'
13  gem 'devise', '~> 3.4.1'
14
15  group :development, :test do
16    gem 'sqlite3'
17  end
```

```
18
19  group :production do
20    gem 'pg',         '0.17.1'
21    gem 'rails_12factor', '0.0.2'
22  end
23
```

So we've done two things here. First, we **REMOVED** the original reference to the gem 'sqlite3' that was in there from when we started our project. We still want to reference it, but we do that by adding it to the group reference on line 15.

That 'group' reference is basically telling our app to use sqlite3 in our development and test environment (remember, we won't be doing any test environment stuff in this book).

Second, we added the postgres database (pg) and rails_12factor (which you need to add with it for Heroku), and designated those to be used in our production environment.

Whenever we add Gems to our Gemfile we need to run bundle install, but this time it needed to be a little different. We needed to run bundle install without production. If you think about that; it makes sense, because we don't want to install the postgres database in our development environment. Here's the command:

```
1  $ bundle install --without production
2
```

Note: that 'without' has two dashes in front of it --

We only need to run that special bundle install command once; Rails will remember from now on not to install production stuff.

Why am I talking about all of this again? Because I want to make sure that you understand that we are using <u>two separate databases</u>. It's important to keep that in mind.

Why? Because whenever we run a migration, we're only pushing that migration into our local database, not our production database. We also need to push it into the production database (postgres in this case) up on Heroku.

PUSHING MIGRATIONS TO POSTGRES AT HEROKU

Stick with me here... when we ran the $ rails generate devise user command we created a migration for our users. Then, when we ran the $ rake db:migrate command we pushed that migration into our database...that is, into our *sqlite3* database.

We haven't pushed it into our Postgres database sitting up at Heroku; and we need to do that. Every time you push a new migration to the local development environment database (sqlite3), you ALSO need to push the migration to your production environment database (postgres). You do that with this command:

```
1  $ heroku run rake db:migrate
2
```

That looks an awful lot like the "rake db:migrate" command we use locally, it just slaps a "heroku run" to the front of it. Just remember that if you don't run this command, your database won't work on Heroku.

CHECK OUT OUR NEW DEVISE WEB PAGES

Alright! We've now completed the Devise installation, we've run our Users migration so Devise can keep track of all the users in both our development and production environments, and we've generated the Views that create the pages that allow people to log in and out and all that good stuff.

So let's take a look at those pages!

First, be sure to stop your web server and restart it.

Next, to find out where those pages are, we need to find the routes that Devise has generated for each of them. So let's run our trusty rake routes command:

```
1  $ rake routes
2
```

Remember the last time we ran this command, we only had two pages in our app (index and about). Now there's a whole bunch of stuff listed there!

```
1  $ rake routes
2  Prefix            Verb      URI Pattern              Controller#Action
3  new_user_session GET   /users/sign_in(.:format)     devise/sessions#new
4  user_session      POST /users/sign_in(.:format)     devise/sessions#create
5  .
6  .
7
```

Just like earlier, the first column is the route. The second is whether it's a web page (GET), a form submission (POST), or a logout (DELETE). The third column is the

URL pattern, and we'll use that to navigate to the page in our web browser. The fourth column is the Controller Action.

I didn't print the whole list here, just the first couple of listings, but you can run the rake routes command yourself and see the full list.

Remember, the ones listed as GET generally tend to be web pages. So let's pick one of them and punch it into our web browser and see what it looks like!

https://pinterested-codemy.c9.io/users/sign_up (or whatever your url is)

(https://pinterested-codemy.c9.io/users/sign_up - Devise User Sign Up Page)

Check out the Login page (/users/sign_in):
https://pinterested-codemy.c9.io/users/sign_in (or whatever your url is)

(https://pinterested-codemy.c9.io/users/sign_in - Devise Users Sign In Page)

There's a link on that page for people who have forgotten their password and need it sent to them, you can check that out as well.

These pages and the forms on them are fully functional. You can now sign up for an account, sign in etc. Sure, the pages look a little lame, but the functionality works and we'll spruce up how they look next.

STYLING DEVISE VIEWS

So let's dive in and make these pages look a little better. It's fairly easy to do. All of the files that we need to edit are located in your /app/views/devise/ folder. Let's start by editing the page that allows people to sign up for an account:

/app/views/devise/registrations/new.html.erb

```
1   <h2>Sign up</h2>
2
3   <%= form_for(resource, as: resource_name, url: registration_path(resource_name)) do |f| %>
4     <%= devise_error_messages! %>
5
```

```
6   <div class="field">
7     <%= f.label :email %><br />
8     <%= f.email_field :email, autofocus: true %>
9   </div>
10
11  <div class="field">
12    <%= f.label :password %>
13    <% if @validatable %>
14    <em>(<%= @minimum_password_length %> characters minimum)</em>
15    <% end %><br />
16    <%= f.password_field :password, autocomplete: "off" %>
17  </div>
18
19  <div class="field">
20    <%= f.label :password_confirmation %><br />
21    <%= f.password_field :password_confirmation, autocomplete: "off" %>
22  </div>
23
24  <div class="actions">
25    <%= f.submit "Sign up" %>
26  </div>
27  <% end %>
28
29  <%= render "devise/shared/links" %>
30
```

This may be the most complicated looking file we've seen so far, but it's not that bad. To edit these Devise views, we're going to use Bootstrap (of course!).

Head over to GetBootstrap.com and click the CSS tab at the top of the screen; then click the "Forms" link on the right-hand side of the screen. There are a couple of things we need to do. We won't be copying and pasting all the code below the example form at GetBootstrap.com, instead we'll just pick out two pieces.

First, Bootstrap wants us to wrap each input field and label in a form-group div:

```
1  <div class="form-group">
2    .
3    .
4  </div>
```

Our new.html.erb file already wraps those things in a div, but it names the div class as "field". You can see this on line 6, 11, and 19 above.

No problem, just replace "field" with "form-group on lines 6, 11, and 19 above.

Second, Bootstrap wants us to add a "form-control" class to each input field. (the input field is the box that you type stuff in on the web form). In our new.html.erb file above, those are located on line 8, 16, and 21:

```
7
8    <%= f.email_field :email, autofocus: true, class: 'form-control' %>
9

15
16  <%= f.password_field :password, autocomplete: "off", class: 'form-control' %>
17

20
21  <%= f.password_field :password_confirmation, autocomplete: "off", class: 'form-control' %>
22
```

Third, notice how our form makes people type in a password, and then type in that password again to confirm it? I don't really think we need people to double type their password for our simple app, so I'm going to remove that. All we have to do is erase lines 19 thru 22.

Fourth, what about the 'Submit' button? It looks a little bland...we can use a Bootstrap button like we've used on our Index page. Let's do that:

```
24
25   <%= f.submit "Sign up", class: 'btn btn-primary' %>
26
```

So here's what our updated file should look like now:

/app/views/devise/registrations/new.html.erb

```
1    <h2>Sign up</h2>
2
3    <%= form_for(resource, as: resource_name, url: registration_path(resource_name)) do |f| %>
4      <%= devise_error_messages! %>
5
6    <div class="form-group">
7      <%= f.label :email %><br />
8      <%= f.email_field :email, autofocus: true, class: 'form-control' %>
9    </div>
10
11    <div class="form-group">
12      <%= f.label :password %>
13      <% if @validatable %>
14      <em>(<%= @minimum_password_length %> characters minimum)</em>
15      <% end %><br />
16      <%= f.password_field :password, autocomplete: "off", class: 'form-control' %>
17    </div>
18
19
20    <div class="actions">
21      <%= f.submit "Sign up", class: 'btn btn-primary' %>
22    </div>
23    <% end %>
```

24
25 <%= render "devise/shared/links" %>
26

(https://pinterested-codemy.c9.io/users/sign_up - Devise User Sign Up Page)

So this definitely looks better, but we can do even better by adding panels. Head back to GetBootstrap.com, click the "Components" link, and then click the "Panels" link on the right-hand side of the screen.

We want to add a "Panel with heading", and we'll also put a "Panel with footing" at the bottom where our "login" link is. Here's how:

/app/views/devise/registrations/new.html.erb

```
1   <div class="panel panel-default">
2     <div class="panel-heading"><h2>Sign up</h2></div>
3     <div class="panel-body">
4
5   <%= form_for(resource, as: resource_name, url: registration_path(resource_name)) do |f| %>
6     <%= devise_error_messages! %>
7
8     <div class="form-group">
```

```
9    <%= f.label :email %><br />
10     <%= f.email_field :email, autofocus: true, class: 'form-control' %>
11   </div>
12
13   <div class="form-group">
14     <%= f.label :password %>
15     <% if @validatable %>
16     <em>(<%= @minimum_password_length %> characters minimum)</em>
17     <% end %><br />
18     <%= f.password_field :password, autocomplete: "off", class: 'form-control' %>
19   </div>
20
21
22   <div class="actions">
23     <%= f.submit "Sign up", class: 'btn btn-primary' %>
24   </div>
25 <% end %>
26   </div>
27   <div class="panel-footer"><%= render "devise/shared/links" %></div>
28 </div>
29
```

You can see the changes in bold. Basically we wrapped the whole page in a div with class="panel panel-default", wrapped the page header in a div with class="panel-heading", wrapped the main meat and potatoes of the page in a div with class="panel-body", and then wrapped the links at the body of the page in a div with class="panel-footer".

The result should look like this:

(https://pinterested-codemy.c9.io/users/sign_up - Devise User Sign Up Page Finished Layout)

You can go through yourself and make these exact same changes to the other Devise views that have forms:

/app/views/devise/registrations/edit.html.erb (lets users edit their profile)

/app/views/devise/sessions/new.html.erb (lets users log in)

/app/views/devise/passwords/new.html.erb (forgotten password page)

You'll notice that those pages all look similar, so you should be able to duplicate the changes we just made to our /app/views/devise/registrations/new.html.erb to each of them.

ADDING LINKS TO DEVISE PAGES

So now we've got our Devise pages looking pretty good, now we need to add links to those pages into our Navbar at the top of each page. We'll add those links using the Ruby link_to tag like we've done in the past, but this time we'll add a little twist.

We aren't going to want to show links to all of the devise pages to all of the people who visit our site. For instance, we don't want to show a link to the "Edit User" page on our Navbar if the person viewing the site has not logged in yet (or isn't even a user!).

Similarly, we don't need to show a link to the login page after a person has already logged in.

And finally, we need to add a link to log out, and that link looks a little different than other links we've created in the past.

DETERMINING WHETHER A USER IS LOGGED IN OR NOT

So first things first, how can we determine whether a user is already logged in or not? Luckily it's pretty easy in rails, we'll just use a bit of Ruby code and a simple "If" statement.

It will basically say "If a user is logged in, show these links, if not – show these other links". Here's the code:

```
1  <% if user_signed_in? %>
2    .
3    .
```

```
4  <% else %>
5     .
6     .
7  <% end %>
8
```

The links that we want to appear only when a user is signed in (edit profile, logout) are listed right after line one and before the "else" statement. The links that we'd like to appear when a user is not signed in (login, sign up) go after the "else" statement and before the "end" statement.

To get the paths to the different pages we'd like to add (edit profile, logout, login, sign up) we can run our trusty rake routes command:

```
1  $ rake routes
2
```

And pay special attention to the ones listed as "GET" (remember to slap a _path to the end for our link_to Ruby code:

Log In:	new_user_session_path
Edit Profile:	edit_user_registration_path
Sign Up:	new_user_registration_path
Log Out:	destroy_user_session_path

Let's look at the last one, the Log Out path. When you run the rake routes command, you'll see it listed as DELETE, not GET. This makes a certain amount of sense because logging out is basically "deleting a session".

But creating a link to a DELETE event is a little different than a regular link. It looks like this:

```
1  <%= link_to 'Logout', destroy_user_session_path, method: :delete %>
2
```

You'll notice the link is the same, except we slapped a "method: :delete" bit to the end. Pretty simple.

UPDATING THE NAVBAR

So now we've got our If statement lined up, and we've got the paths to the new Devise pages that we'd like to add. Let's update our Navbar:

/app/views/home/_header.html.erb
```
1  <nav class="navbar navbar-default" role="navigation">
2   <div class="container">
3   <!-- Brand and toggle get grouped for better mobile display -->
4   <div class="navbar-header">
5           <button type="button" class="navbar-toggle collapsed" data-
6   toggle="collapse" data-target="#bs-example-navbar-collapse-1">
7     <span class="sr-only">Toggle navigation</span>
8     <span class="icon-bar"></span>
9     <span class="icon-bar"></span>
10    <span class="icon-bar"></span>
11   </button>
12   <%= link_to 'Pinterested', root_path, class: 'navbar-brand' %>
13   </div>
14
15   <!-- Collect the nav links, forms, and other content for toggling -->
16   <div class="collapse navbar-collapse" id="bs-example-navbar-collapse-1">
```

```
17    <ul class="nav navbar-nav navbar-right">
18      <li><%= link_to 'Home', root_path %></li>
19      <li><%= link_to 'About Me', home_about_path %></li>
20
21      <% if user_signed_in? %>
22        <li><%= link_to 'Edit Profile', edit_user_registration_path %></li>
23        <li><%= link_to 'Logout', destroy_user_session_path, method: :delete %></li>
24      <% else %>
25        <li><%= link_to "Login", new_user_session_path %></li>
26        <li><%= link_to "Join", new_user_registration_path %></li>
27      <% end %>
28    </ul>
29    </div><!-- /.navbar-collapse -->
30  </div><!-- /.container-fluid -->
31 </nav>
32
```

So the changes are lines 21 through 27. Notice we put the IF statement that checks whether a user is signed in or not AFTER the first two links (Home and About) because we want those two links to show up if a user is signed in or not signed in.

We're moving right along. We can add new users, log in, log out, update user profiles, and our Navbar now shows links dynamically based on whether a user is logged in or out.

Now it's time to start adding *real* functionality to our site and allow people to start uploading pinterest style "pins", and that's what we'll do in the next chapter.

CHAPTER FIVE

BUILDING A SCAFFOLD

We're getting down to the meat and potatoes of our app now. In this chapter we're going to start to build out the main functionality for our site.

Let's break down that functionality…

Since we're building a Pinterest clone, we're going to want to be able to upload a 'pin' that consists of an image, and a written description. We'll need to store that information in our database and show that information on the website.

Rails (of course) has something that will take care of all of that for us, and it's called a scaffold. A Rails scaffold creates a model, a migration, controllers to handle everything, and views to see and manipulate things.

To create a scaffold, we just need to issue one simple command:

```
1  $ rails g scaffold pins description:string
2
```

We've seen a similar command when we set up Devise. 'rails g' stands for 'rails generate', so this command is telling Rails to generate a scaffold named 'pins'.

We can name our scaffold anything, but sticking with our pinterest theme, we'll name ours 'pins'. We could just as easily have named it horses, or tweets, or posts. The convention is to name it something plural (ending in an s).

The command ends with 'description:string'. That tells Rails to create a column in our database called description, and to give that description a string data type.

When dealing with database stuff, you will generally work with either strings (which is a short string of characters or text), integers (whole numbers), decimals (decimal numbers), or maybe text (longer text like paragraphs). Possible data types include:

:binary
:boolean
:date
:datetime
:decimal
:float
:integer
:primary_key
:references
:string
:text
:time
:timestamp

We don't really need to know what all of those are right now, you can do a little research in the future as you grow as a Rails developer.

The 'rails g scaffold' command creates a migration, and like all migrations we'll need to rake our database to push the migration up to the database:

```
1  $ rake db:migrate
2
```

And later when we push these changes up to Heroku, we'll need to run Heroku's rake db:migrate command:

```
1   $ heroku run rake db:migrate
2
```

When you ran the 'rails g scaffold' command, you probably noticed that the command line outputted a bunch of things that Rails just created for you. You'll notice that there's a new folder in your views directory called /pins/.

Before we look through those files, we need to restart our server and check out our website because something strange has happened.

Head over to **https://pinterested-codemy.c9.io** (or whatever your URL is)

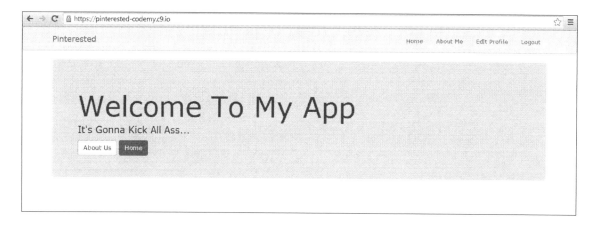

(https://pinterested-codemy.c9.io – After Scaffold)

Reload the page. Notice anything different? Everything should look a little 'off'. The font is a slightly different size, the buttons look just a little different, and everything seems…somehow wrong.

What happened? Whenever we generate a scaffold in Rails, one of the files that gets created is a CSS file for the scaffold! That CSS file is over-writing our Bootstrap CSS file (the one we created and named bootstraply.css.scss).

So take a look at the /app/assets/stylesheets directory and you should see the new stylesheet, named: /app/assets/stylesheets/scaffolds.css.scss

If you want, you can open that file and just take a look at it for fun, but what we need to do is simply delete it. You can do that by putting your mouse over the file name right there on the directory tree on the left-hand side of your development environment, right-clicking, and selecting "Delete".

Now if we head back to our website and hit reload, the site should look the way it did earlier under Bootstrap.

CHECKING OUT THE SCAFFOLD VIEWS

The 'rails g scaffold' command that we ran created a bunch of files for us, so let's take a look at all of them now by running our trusty rake routes command:

```
1  $ rake routes
2
```

At the top of the list you should see a bunch of routes marked 'pins'. Pay special attention to the GET routes as those are generally the ones that create pages on our website.

You should see:

pins
new_pin
edit_pin
pin

The one we want to focus on right now is 'pins', in fact; you can head to your website and take a look at it right now:

https://pinterested-codemy.c9.io/pins (or whatever your URL is)

(https://pinterested-codemy.c9.io/pins)

As you can see, there isn't much there yet, because we haven't added any actual pins yet. But you can see the link that says "New Pin" and if you click on it, you'll find a page where you can create and upload a pin.

(https://pinterested-codemy.c9.io/pins/new)

The only thing that the form asks for is the "Description", and that's because when we ran our 'rails g scaffold' command, the only item we listed was description:string.

"But, I thought we would be making pins with images?!" yeah – yeah, one step at a time! Right now I just want to show you how to get things rolling with a simple description; we'll add images soon.

So create a pin. Type in something into the description field and click the "Create Pin" button. Then head back to:

https://pinterested-codemy.c9.io/pins (or whatever your URL is)

You should see your pin listed there. Go ahead and create a few more pins, just to get things rolling:

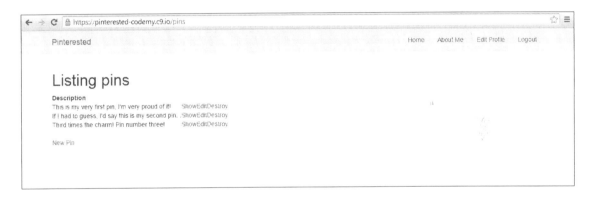

(https://pinterested-codemy.c9.io/pins - with a few pins added)

All your pins are listed on the pins page in a simple table. But notice next to each pin there are three links: "Show, Edit, Destroy". Those links do exactly what you would think they would do.

Go ahead and play around with them a bit…I'll wait.

THAT'S CRUD!

Before we move on, we need to discuss something that's very fundamental to web development, and that's CRUD.

Create
Read
Update
Destroy

We've just generated a simple scaffold, but that tool is one of the most powerful things you'll ever come across in web development. Why? Because that simple scaffold has given us the tools and ability to handle CRUD (Create, Read, Update, and Destroy).

You can see in our simple Pinterest app that we now have the ability to Create something (a simple pin with description text). We can View that pin (Read it), we can edit it (Update it), and we can delete it (Destroy it). CRUD.

So what?

Take a minute and think about every major website in the Internet. Don't they pretty much all just do CRUD?

Think about Twitter...it's a massive website, but when you get right down to it, when you use Twitter, you're only really Creating a Tweet, Reading a Tweet, Updating a Tweet, or Deleting a Tweet...CRUD!

What about Facebook? Create a Facebook post, Read a Facebook Post, Update a Facebook Post, or Delete a Facebook Post...CRUD!

Youtube? Create a Video Post, Watch a Video (read), Updating one of your videos, or Delete a Video...CRUD!

What about a Blog? You create a blog post, read a blog post, update your blog post, or delete your blog post...CRUD!

Everything, and I mean *everything* basically just breaks down to CRUD. It's one of the fundamental building blocks of the Internet and we just learned how to handle it with one simple command in Rails.

One simple command and Rails handles *everything* about it! It's really pretty amazing, and it gives you an incredible tool that you can use to build just about anything online.

Sure, our simple pin description isn't much right now...but we'll tinker with it a bit and make it more impressive (adding images etc).

Right now, I just want you to focus on CRUD, and how the Rails g Scaffold command has given you the ability to create CRUD. We have more to learn, but this is the first step and it's a big one.

SCAFFOLD VIEWS AND CONTROLLER

Let's take a minute to look at some of the files that the 'rails g scaffold' command created. As I mentioned, you should have a new 'pins' folder in your /views/ directory. There should be six or seven files in that folder (some of which you can ignore – like the json ones).

The other files are the pages that allow us to create pins (new.html.erb), edit pins (edit.html.erb), show an individual pin (show.html.erb), and list all the pins (index.html.erb).

If you take a look at those files, you'll notice that most of them call a partial file to handle the actual form used to create a pin or edit the pin:

```
1  <%= render 'form' %>
2
```

That form partial file is also located in the pins folder, and is named _form.html.erb

You can go through those files (both the views and the form partial) and play with the look of them. I'll leave it as homework for you to make them look the same as our Devise views (use the Bootstrap 'form' class and 'panel' class like we used for our Devise views).

Besides the views, the 'rails g scaffold' command also created a new controller to handle all of this CRUD stuff. The controller is located in /app/controllers/pins_controller.rb and should look like this:

/app/controllers/pins_controller.rb

```
1   class PinsController < ApplicationController
2     before_action :set_pin, only: [:show, :edit, :update, :destroy]
3
4     respond_to :html
5
6     def index
7       @pins = Pin.all
8       respond_with(@pins)
9     end
10
11    def show
12      respond_with(@pin)
13    end
14
15    def new
16      @pin = Pin.new
17      respond_with(@pin)
```

```ruby
18   end
19
20   def edit
21   end
22
23   def create
24     @pin = Pin.new(pin_params)
25     @pin.save
26     respond_with(@pin)
27   end
28
29   def update
30     @pin.update(pin_params)
31     respond_with(@pin)
32   end
33
34   def destroy
35     @pin.destroy
36     respond_with(@pin)
37   end
38
39   private
40     def set_pin
41       @pin = Pin.find(params[:id])
42     end
43
44     def pin_params
45       params.require(:pin).permit(:description)
46     end
47   end
48
```

That's quite a bit more stuff than our old home_controller.rb file that we created back at the beginning of this book when we made our original index and about page! But it makes sense that this file would be a little more complicated, since this controller needs to handle all the CRUD stuff.

Take a look through this controller file. You don't need to understand everything that's going on in there at this point...but you should get at least a small sense of what's happening.

Look at the different 'def' sections. Notice how they sort of follow along with CRUD? There's a 'def show' (Read from CRUD), there's a 'def new' and 'def create' (Create from CRUD), there's a 'def edit' and 'def update' (Update from Crud), and a 'def destroy' (Destroy from CRUD).

Apart from that; there's some stuff towards the bottom, private and 'def pins_params' that we'll fiddle with later.

Like I said though, you don't really need to know what all this is doing at the moment, but you need to have a sense of it and realize that this controller is handling our CRUD stuff for us.

ADDED TABLE TO OUR DATABASE

Our database is getting more and more complicated. Earlier, all it did was handle users signing up, logging in and out, and editing their profiles. Now it has to handle all of the pins that people upload.

Luckily, Rails still handles all this database stuff for us behind the scenes, but we can take a look at a sort of snapshot of what our database looks like by checking out our database schema file, located at: /app/db/schema.rb

You'll remember that the /app/db/ directory is where our migration files are located, so it makes sense that this is where our schema.rb file is located.

Basically a schema.rb file is just a snapshot of our current database. You won't need to ever do anything with this file (you won't need to edit it or anything), but it's nice to take a quick peek at it from time to time. Let's do so now…

/app/db/schema.rb

```
1   ActiveRecord::Schema.define(version: 20141229144241) do
2
3     create_table "pins", force: true do |t|
4       t.string   "description"
5       t.datetime "created_at"
6       t.datetime "updated_at"
7     end
8
9     create_table "users", force: true do |t|
10      t.string   "email",              default: "", null: false
11      t.string   "encrypted_password", default: "", null: false
12      t.string   "reset_password_token"
13      t.datetime "reset_password_sent_at"
14      t.datetime "remember_created_at"
15      t.integer  "sign_in_count",      default: 0,  null: false
16      t.datetime "current_sign_in_at"
17      t.datetime "last_sign_in_at"
18      t.string   "current_sign_in_ip"
19      t.string   "last_sign_in_ip"
20      t.datetime "created_at"
21      t.datetime "updated_at"
22    end
23
24    add_index "users", ["email"], name: "index_users_on_email", unique: true
25    add_index "users", ["reset_password_token"], name:
26    "index_users_on_reset_password_token", unique: true
```

```
27
28  end
29
```

You'll notice that there are two tables in our database; one to handle all the Devise things ("users"), and one to handle all our pins stuff ("pins").

You'll also notice that both tables have timestamp information that was created automatically when we created the table (Rails does that for us – for instance, in our "pins" table we only wanted it to add a description:string, but our pins table also has a t.datetime "created_at" column and a t.datetime "updated_at" column).

Like I said, there's nothing we need to do here, I just wanted to make you aware of the schema.rb file. You should get into the habit of taking a look at that file every time you make any sort of change to the database (anytime you push a migration, for instance)… just to keep an eye on things.

CHECK OUT OUR PINS INDEX PAGE

Finally, let's take a moment to check out our main pins index page. This is going to become one of the most important files of our site, because this is where we're going to do most of the work to make our site look and feel like pinterest. Let's take a look at what we have there so far:

/app/views/pins/index.html.erb

```
1  <h1>Listing pins</h1>
2
3  <table>
4    <thead>
5      <tr>
```

```
6     <th>Description</th>
7     <th colspan="3"></th>
8   </tr>
9  </thead>
10
11  <tbody>
12    <% @pins.each do |pin| %>
13     <tr>
14      <td><%= pin.description %></td>
15      <td><%= link_to 'Show', pin %></td>
16      <td><%= link_to 'Edit', edit_pin_path(pin) %></td>
17       <td><%= link_to 'Destroy', pin, method: :delete, data: { confirm: 'Are you
18         sure?' } %></td>
19     </tr>
20    <% end %>
21  </tbody>
22 </table>
23
24 <br/>
25
26 <%= link_to 'New Pin', new_pin_path %>
27
```

You'll notice the main layout of the page is a basic HTML table. If you don't have a lot of experience with HTML and aren't familiar with tables, don't worry. We won't be keeping the table (eventually we'll remove the table and use Bootstrap panels to make each 'pin' look like a pinterest pin).

The most interesting stuff happens on lines 12-20. Those are the lines that call into our database, look up our pins table, and output each pin onto the screen.

Line 12 is a basic Ruby loop <% @pins.each do |pin| %> that says "for each pin in our pins table, do something"; and the 'something' are lines 14-18 (ie output the pin.description and links to show, edit, or destroy the pin).

The reference to pin.description is the description:string that our 'rails g scaffold pins description:string" command generated (ie each pin's description).

We'll play with this file again soon; when we finally add images into the mix.

UPDATING THE NAVBAR

Now that we have a few more pages in our site, it's time to update the Navbar with links to those pages; specifically the pins index page and the 'add new' pin page:

https://pinterested-codemy.c9.io/pins (or whatever your URL is)
https://pinterested-codemy.c9.io/pins/new

We don't mind showing the world our pins index page, but we probably only want people who are signed in to be able to directly access the "add new" pin page (in the next chapter we'll get into authentication). Remember how we split the Navbar up based on whether a user is signed in or not?

/app/views/home/_header.html.erb
```
1  <nav class="navbar navbar-default" role="navigation">
2    <div class="container">
3      <!-- Brand and toggle get grouped for better mobile display -->
4      <div class="navbar-header">
5                <button type="button" class="navbar-toggle collapsed" data-
6      toggle="collapse" data-target="#bs-example-navbar-collapse-1">
7        <span class="sr-only">Toggle navigation</span>
8        <span class="icon-bar"></span>
```

```
9      <span class="icon-bar"></span>
10     <span class="icon-bar"></span>
11    </button>
12    <%= link_to 'Pinterested', root_path, class: 'navbar-brand' %>
13   </div>
14
15   <!-- Collect the nav links, forms, and other content for toggling -->
16   <div class="collapse navbar-collapse" id="bs-example-navbar-collapse-1">
17     <ul class="nav navbar-nav navbar-right">
18       <li><%= link_to 'Home', root_path %></li>
19       <li><%= link_to 'About Me', home_about_path %></li>
20       <li><%= link_to 'List Pins', pins_path %></li>
21       <% if user_signed_in? %>
22         <li><%= link_to 'Edit Profile', edit_user_registration_path %></li>
23         <li><%= link_to 'Add Pin', new_pin_path %></li>
23         <li><%= link_to 'Logout', destroy_user_session_path, method: :delete %></li>
24       <% else %>
25         <li><%= link_to "Login", new_user_session_path %></li>
26         <li><%= link_to "Join", new_user_registration_path %></li>
27       <% end %>
28     </ul>
29   </div><!-- /.navbar-collapse -->
30   </div><!-- /.container-fluid -->
31  </nav>
32
```

We've done a lot in this chapter! Be sure to save your changes:

```
1  $ git add .
2  $ git commit –am 'added pins scaffold, updated navbar'
3  $ git push
4  $ git push heroku master
5  $ heroku run rake db:migrate
6
```

Be sure to run the rake db:migrate command on Heroku since we added a new element to our database (the pins table).

In the next chapter we'll look at Authentication and set up safeguards that only allow signed-in users to add pins to our database.

CHAPTER SIX

AUTHENTICATING USERS

In the last chapter we laid down the foundation of our pins scaffold. Now people have the ability to upload basic pins and describe them.

But there's a problem. Right now, *anyone* can create a pin. Not only that, but anyone can edit a pin or delete a pin...even if they didn't create that pin themselves!

That's definitely not going to fly. We need to set things up so that only people who have signed-up and signed-in can create pins, and only people who created a specific pin should have the ability to edit it or delete it.

How do we do this? The first part is easy (only giving people who have signed-in the ability to create pins). The second part is a little trickier; we need to "associate" a user with a pin.

RAILS ASSOCIATIONS

Right now our app has two models (in the database)...one for 'users' and one for 'pins'. When we looked at our database schema in the last chapter, you saw how each of those is a separate table in our database.

The thing is; we now want to *associate* those two models. We want to be able to keep track of which pins belong to which user. Luckily Rails makes this pretty easy with something called "Associations".

In Rails, there are a few basic types of associations available to you:

- belongs_to
- has_one
- has_many
- has_many :through
- has_one :through
- has_and_belongs_to_many

Each of these associations can refer to a model in our app (in our case, let's look at our pins model). We mainly want to focus on the first three:

A pin can *"belong to"* a user.

A user can *"have one"* pin.

A user can *"have many"* pins.

The other three listed above are for more complicated associations that we don't really need to understand for our simple app. But you can read a great rails guide about each of these associations at:

http://guides.rubyonrails.org/association_basics.html

USING ASSOCIATIONS

Setting up associations is fairly easy. In our app we need to use the "belongs_to" and the "has_many" associations. We don't need to use the "has_one" association because we want our users to be able to have as many pins as they want, and the has_many allows one or more than one.

WARNING – WARNING – WARNING!

Before we go forward, it's important to delete any pins you've already created; both on the development version and the Heroku version of your app. Why? Because we're going to start associating pins with users, and any pins you've already created have not been associated with a user and will throw up errors after we set our associations.

So delete all the pins that are currently listed on your pins index page. There's a way to associate our old pins with users later using the Rails Console, but it's easier to just delete them now.

It's also probably a good idea to close your user account on the site. Log in, click the 'edit profile' link at the top of the screen, and click the "cancel my account" button at the bottom of the page.

CREATING ASSOCIATIONS

Using associations is a two-step process. We need to specify the associations in each of our models at /app/models/pin.rb and /app/models/user.rb but we also need to add a new column to our pins table (in our database) to keep track of what pins belong to what user.

Let's do that first.

We can edit a table by creating a migration and pushing that migration to the database with the rake db:migrate command. In this case, we want to add a user_id column to our pins table and make it an integer data type.

To do that we issue this command:

```
1  $ rails generate migration add_user_id_to_pins user_id:integer:index
2
```

This command looks familiar but seems a little different. The different part is the add_user_id_to_pins bit. It looks a little weird but that's how you tell Rails to add a column to a table (in this case, we're adding a user_id to the pins table).

The last bit looks similar to when we designated description:string for our original pins table, but in this case we're creating a user_id and making it an integer (number).

But we've also tacked on an :index to the end. An index in database-world just makes a thing easier and faster to look up. It speeds up the lookup process and you don't really need to know more than that for now.

So run that command, and then rake the database:

```
1  $ rake db:migrate
2
```

(be sure to remember to run 'heroku run rake db:migrate' later when you push all these changes up to Heroku).

If you take a look at our database schema file now, you'll notice that our pins table now has a user_id with integer data type.

The next thing to do is actually specify our associations. We do that in our two /app/models/ files (pin.rb and user.rb).

/app/models/pin.rb

```
1   class Pin < ActiveRecord::Base
2     belongs_to :user
3   end
4
```

/app/models/user.rb

```
1   class User < ActiveRecord::Base
2     # Include default devise modules. Others available are:
3     # :confirmable, :lockable, :timeoutable and :omniauthable
4     devise :database_authenticatable, :registerable,
5     :recoverable, :rememberable, :trackable, :validatable
6     has_many :pins
7   end
8
```

You see that adding associations is as simple as adding one line to each model. Piece of cake!

MUST BE SIGNED IN TO CREATE PINS

Finally, we mentioned at the beginning of this chapter that we only want people who are signed in to be able to create pins.

This is easily accomplished by tweaking our pins controller file, and adding a couple of lines to the top of it:

/app/controllers/pins_controller.rb

```
1   class PinsController < ApplicationController
2     before_action :set_pin, only: [:show, :edit, :update, :destroy]
3     before_action :authenticate_user!, except: [:index, :show]
4     before_action :correct_user, only: [:edit, :update, :destroy]
5   .
6   .
7
```

Lines 3 and 4 are what we're looking at...

Line three authenticates a user for every page of our app (relating to pins) except the index and show pages. So a user doesn't have to be logged in to view our pins index page or an individual pin.

Line four makes sure that only the correct user can edit, update, or destroy a pin. But we need to specify what is a correct user. We'll do that at the very bottom of this same file, before the final end statement:

/app/controllers/pins_controller.rb

```
1   .
2   .
3   def correct_user
4       @pin = current_user.pins.find_by(id: params[:id])
5       redirect_to pins_path, notice: "Not authorized to edit this pin" if @pin.nil?
6   end
7
```

Notice line four mentions current_user; that is something called a 'Devise Helper' (something that Devise handles for us). Basically it allows us to reference who the current logged in user is.

Whenever someone creates a new pin, we need to be able to let our database know that specific pin belongs to that specific user, and we'll use the current_user bit we just saw to do that.

So basically we need to update the 'def new' section and the 'def create' section of our pins controller and replace Pin.new with current_user.pins.build in each of them.

So here's what our new pins controller looks like:

/app/controllers/pins_controller.rb

```
1   class PinsController < ApplicationController
2   before_action :set_pin, only: [:show, :edit, :update, :destroy]
3   before_action :authenticate_user!, except: [:index, :show]
4   before_action :correct_user, only: [:edit, :update, :destroy]
5
6    respond_to :html
7
8    def index
9      @pins = Pin.all
10   end
11
12   def show
13   end
14
15   def new
16     @pin = current_user.pins.build
17   end
18
19   def edit
20   end
21
22   def create
23     @pin = current_user.pins.build(pin_params)
```

```ruby
24    if @pin.save
25      redirect_to @pin, notice: 'Pin was successfully created.'
26    else
27      render action: 'new'
28    end
29  end
30
31  def update
32   if @pin.update(pin_params)
33      redirect_to @pin, notice: 'Pin was successfully updated.'
34    else
35      render action: 'edit'
36    end
37  end
38
39  def destroy
40    @pin.destroy
41    redirect_to pins_url
42  end
43
44  private
45   def set_pin
46     @pin = Pin.find(params[:id])
47   end
48
49   def pin_params
50     params.require(:pin).permit(:description)
51   end
52
53  def correct_user
54     @pin = current_user.pins.find_by(id: params[:id])
55     redirect_to pins_path, notice: "Not authorized to edit this pin" if @pin.nil?
56   end
57
```

58 end
59

You'll see that I also added a couple of lines to output a flash message notice when a pin is updated or created.

We're almost done. The heavy lifting is over, but we still need to make a cosmetic change or two to our website.

Before we continue be sure to close your web server and restart your app. Otherwise you'll probably get an error.

Once you've done that, create a new user account (since you deleted yours at the beginning of this chapter), and log back in. Then check out our pins index page:

https://pinterested-codemy.c9.io/pins (or whatever your URL is)

That page should be blank since we deleted all of our pins, but go ahead and add another pin. Notice next to the pin we still have the "show, edit, destroy" links.

That's fine because you are currently logged in and those pins are yours…but we don't really want the edit and destroy links to show up if a person isn't logged in or doesn't own that particular pin.

It's sort of a moot point right now. To see what I mean, log out and then check out the pins page. Try to click the edit or destroy link and you'll get a message saying that you need to log in to perform those operations.

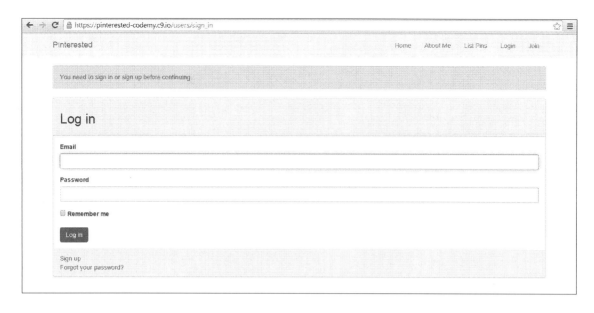

(After clicking on 'add new', 'edit', or 'destroy' pin link while logged out)

So strictly speaking, our app is locked down now and authenticating users appropriately. But still…it's kind of silly to show those links to people who can't actually use them.

Luckily we can change that pretty easily by adding a simple Ruby 'If Statement':

/app/views/pins/index.html.erb

```
1  .
2  .
3  <% @pins.each do |pin| %>
4      <tr>
5        <td><%= pin.description %></td>
6        <td><%= link_to 'Show', pin %></td>
7        <% if pin.user == current_user %>
8          <td><%= link_to 'Edit', edit_pin_path(pin) %></td>
9          <td><%= link_to 'Destroy', pin, method: :delete, data: { confirm: 'Are you
10           sure?' } %></td>
```

11   **<% end %>**
11   </tr>
12   <% end %>
13

And you can do the same thing to the show.html.erb file with a slight variation:

/app/views/pins/show.html.erb
1   .
2   .
3   <% if @pin.user == current_user %>
4   <%= link_to 'Edit', edit_pin_path(@pin) %>
5   <% end %>
6   <%= link_to 'Back', pins_path %>
7

Those 'If' statements say that 'if' the user that created that pin is the same as our current user, show the edit links, otherwise don't.

That will make sure that only the appropriate people can see the links to edit the pin and will generally make our app less cluttered. There's no reason to add links to a page that a person doesn't have the ability to use anyway.

The reason we slapped an @ sign in fron of pin.user in our show.html.erb file and not in our index.html.erb file is because the index.html.erb file had already called @pin on line 3 (for the loop). The show.html.erb file hadn't called @pins anywhere so we need to do that in order to access the database table.

SUMMING UP

This was a pretty intense chapter, probably the most intense chapter of the entire book. It's ok if you didn't quite understand everything that we did...you'll understand it eventually.

The goal at this point is to know that we did these things, and to be aware of the basic concepts that accompany each thing. Messing with the controller is always tricky when you're first learning Rails, and Associations are an even more advanced topic.

Don't worry; it all gets easier from here!

In the next chapter we'll start adding images to the mix. It should be much more fun!

Before we go on though, be sure to save your work:

```
1  $ git add .
2  $ git commit –am "Associated pins with users and authenticated users"
3  $ git push
4  $ git push heroku master
5  $ heroku run rake db:migrate
6
```

And you should probably delete any pins that have been created as well because we're going to be changing them to show images in the next chapter.

CHAPTER SEVEN

UPLOADING IMAGES TO OUR APP WITH PAPERCLIP

The worst is over! Now we just need to add the ability to upload images, save those images somewhere, style the output to make it look more like Pinterest, and we're basically done!

To handle images, we're going to be working with a few different things; namely ImageMagick, Paperclip, and AmazonS3.

ImageMagick is an open source command line image processing tool. It does all kinds of things behind the scenes like resize images, handle file formats, and all kinds of tricky things like that. It's important because people are going to be uploading images of all different sizes and shapes and we need to be able to resize them into a standard format automatically.

ImageMagick is not an actual Gem, we'll need to download the program into our development environment through the terminal. No worries though, it's easy.

Paperclip is a Ruby Gem that deals with uploading images. Technically it allows for image file attachments to be added to our database. We'll add it like we add all Gems.

Finally, we'll be storing our production level images on Amazon S3 and NOT on our Heroku Postgres database.

Why?

Paperclip has no problem uploading images to postgres databases, but *Heroku* has a problem with it. Image files take up a LOT of space, and Heroku doesn't want to be in the business of storing gazillions of images in their databases.

They'll allow you to upload images into your postgres database, but then in an hour or so those images will be automatically deleted.

So we need to store them somewhere else. Amazon S3 is a simple storage provider that allows you to easily store images in the cloud.

NOTE AmazonS3 does cost money…but it's not much money. For our simple app with just a little traffic and not many images stored, you can expect to pay pennies per month.

Personally, I store a TON of stuff on AmazonS3 and last month my bill was like $1.29… It's cheap.

You don't have to use Amazon S3 for this project if you just don't want to spend the pennies, but I highly recommend that you do because S3 is an industry standard and chances are, you'll have to use them some day for something, and you might as well learn how to now.

But we'll get into that later on in the chapter, first – let's get into ImageMagick.

INSTALLING IMAGEMAGICK

Like I said, ImageMagick is not a Gem, in fact it's not even really a Rails thing. It works with all sorts of web development tools.

To see whether or not ImageMagick is already installed in your development environment, punch this into the terminal:

```
1  $ identify
2
```

If you don't have ImageMagick installed already (and you probably don't), you'll get an error message that says something like "Command not found".

So let's install ImageMagick:

```
1  $ sudo apt-get install imagemagick
2
```

Apt-get is a unix/linux command that downloads and installs software from the command line. It might prompt you; asking if you would like to continue or not. Type yes and hit enter.

Now you can run the identify command and it should output a bunch of stuff. The stuff isn't important, it just tells you that ImageMagick was successfully installed and is ready to go.

That's all there is to it.

INSTALLING PAPERCLIP

Paperclip is a Ruby Gem, so we can head over to RubyGems.org and search for paperclip. As of this book, paperclip is on version 4.2.1, so copy that and add it to our Gemfile:

/Gemfile
```
1  .
2  .
3  gem 'paperclip', '~> 4.2.1'
4  .
5  .
6
```

Save that and then run bundle install as always.

```
1  $ bundle install
2
```

As you might expect, there are a few more things we need to do in order to properly install and use paperclip. We need to make a few changes to the form on our 'add new' pins page, but we also need to make a change to our pins model:

/app/models/pin.rb

```
1   class Pin < ActiveRecord::Base
2     belongs_to :user
3     has_attached_file :image, :styles => { :medium => "300x300>", :thumb => "100x100>" }
4     validates_attachment_content_type :image, :content_type => /\Aimage\/.*\Z/
5   end
6
```

Line 3 and 4 allow our pin model to allow an attached image file, and they go on to specify those images.

Checkout line 3...Notice how it designates a size of medium (300x300) and a size of thumb (100x100). This will allow us to resize images and show them in those standard sizes just by calling :medium or :thumb on our views pages.

Line 4 spells out the type of images that are allowed (jpg, png, bmp, gif, etc). Basically line 4 allows all image types to be uploaded but you could fiddle with that line if, for instance, you only wanted to allow jpg's.

Now we need to create a migration to add a column for images to our pins table:

```
1  $ rails generate paperclip pin image
2
```

And as always, we need to rake the database:

```
1  $ rake db:migrate
2
```

And be sure to do the same thing to Heroku when you finally push these changes up to Heroku (heroku run rake db:migrate).

Now, if you take a look at our database Schema file, you'll notice several references to images in the Pins table.

Finally, we need to make a small change to our pins_controller.rb file to allow images to pass as an accepted parameter on our forms.

/app/controllers/pins_controller.rb
```
1  .
2  .
3  def pin_params
4    params.require(:pin).permit(:description, :image)
5  end
6
```

You'll find that code down towards the end of the file, and we just slapped a comma and :image to the end of it. That whole line means basically "allow people to fill out the form to add a pin by adding a description and uploading an image".

CHANGING OUR WEB FORM TO ALLOW IMAGES

Now we've got the functionality to upload images, but if you go to our 'add new' pins page, you'll notice that there's no form field to actually upload an image. Let's add that now:

/app/views/pins/_form.html.erb

```
1  <%= form_for @pin, html: { multipart: true } do |f| %>
2  .
3  .
4  .
5    <div class="form-group">
6      <%= f.label :image %>
7      <%= f.file_field :image, class: "form-control" %>
8    </div>
9  .
10 .
11
```

You'll notice we did two things here. First, we changed the very first line of the file from:

```
1 <%= form_for(@pin) do |f| %>
2
```

To...

```
1  <%= form_for @pin, html: { multipart: true } do |f| %>
2
```

Basically, we just added a bit that tells our form to allow multipart stuff (ie images).

Next, we added an actual field that allows people to select files from their own computers to upload. Now if we save this file and head over to our web browser:

https://pinterested-codemy.c9.io/pins/new (or whatever your URL is)

You should see this:

(https://pinterested-codemy.c9.io/pins/new - with new Image Field)

Give it a try, you should be able to upload images no problem…

Except that after you upload the images, nothing happens. If you return to our pins index page, there won't be any images listed. We have to update our views to actually SHOW the images now!

To do that, we would call something like this:

```
1  <%= image_tag pin.image.url(:medium) %>
2
```

Notice the :medium? That will output our 300x300 image. You could also have chosen :thumb instead and it will output our 100x100 image.

So let's add that tag to our pins index page and our pins show page:

/app/views/pins/index.html.erb

```
1  <h1>Listing pins</h1>
2
3  <table>
4   <thead>
5    <tr>
6     <th>Image</th>
7     <th>Description</th>
8     <th colspan="3"></th>
9    </tr>
10   </thead>
11
12   <tbody>
13    <% @pins.each do |pin| %>
14     <tr>
15      <td><%= image_tag pin.image.url(:medium) %></td>
16      <td><%= pin.description %></td>
17      <td><%= link_to 'Show', pin %></td>
18      <td><%= link_to 'Edit', edit_pin_path(pin) %></td>
19      <td><%= link_to 'Destroy', pin, method: :delete, data: { confirm: 'Are you
20       sure?' } %></td>
21     </tr>
22    <% end %>
```

```
23   </tbody>
24   </table>
25
26   <br/>
27
28   <%= link_to 'New Pin', new_pin_path %>
29
```

That will output our image on the pins index page, but we still need to update our pins show page:

/app/views/pins/show.html.erb
```
1   <p id="notice"><%= notice %></p>
2
3   <%= image_tag @pin.image.url(:medium) %><br/>
4   <strong>Description:</strong>
5   <%= @pin.description %>
6   <br/>
7
8   <%= link_to 'Edit', edit_pin_path(@pin) %> |
9   <%= link_to 'Back', pins_path %>
10
```

Reload and check it out…if images aren't appearing, then restart your server and hit reload again. That should do the trick.

Check out those two changes, you'll notice that we added a slightly different reference to our image on the pins index page than on the pins show page.

The pins index page image reference (line 15) has no @ sign, and the one on our pins show page (line 3) says @pin.image.url.

What gives?

You'll notice on the pins index page, line 13 already references @pins

```
1  <% @pins.each do |pin| %>
2
```

...and is executing a loop within @pins.

Our pins show page has no loop calling @pins anywhere...so when we call our image, we need to reference @pins.

Let's save our work up until now:

```
1  $ git add .
2  $ git commit –am 'added imagemagick and paperclip, updated pins views'
3  $ git push
4  $ git push heroku master
5  $ heroku run rake db:migrate
6
```

SAVING IMAGES ON AMAZON S3

Now it's time to set up and configure Amazon S3. If you don't have an account at Amazon AWS, head over to aws.amazon.com and sign up for a free account. They'll ask for your credit card, but you only get charged for bandwidth and like I said earlier, it's only going to be pennies a month for our simple app.

Like most things in Rails, there's a Gem to handle AmazonS3 and it is called: "aws-sdk". So head over to RubyGems.org and search for it. As of this book's publication, aws-sdk is on version 1.60.2 so copy the reference to that and add it to our Gemfile:

/Gemfile
```
1  .
2  .
3  gem 'aws-sdk', '~> 1.60.2'
4
```

And as always, we need to run the bundle install command:

```
1  $ bundle install
2
```

We need to make a couple more changes in order to properly configure this gem:

/app/config/environments/production.rb

```
1  .
2  .
3  config.paperclip_defaults = {
4    :storage => :s3,
5    :s3_credentials => {
6    :bucket => ENV['AWS_BUCKET'],
7    :access_key_id => ENV['AWS_ACCESS_KEY_ID'],
8    :secret_access_key => ENV['AWS_SECRET_ACCESS_KEY']
9    }
10   }
11 end
12
```

You'll remember this file from the beginning of the book when we added our Heroku URL. This is the file that gives special instructions for our production environment (ie Heroku).

It makes sense, since we're adding images to Amazon S3 in the production environment, we would have to add a little something to this file to make our app aware of it.

Let's look at the code we added. Basically we are telling paperclip to store images at S3. Now we need three things from S3: bucket name, access_key_id, and secret_access_key.

Let's look at each of these three things.

First, Amazon S3 uses a directory structure to store your files, and it names those directories "buckets". So when you log into S3, you'll create a bucket to store your files in. Our app needs to know the name of that bucket, hence the reference here.

Next, Amazon authenticates our app by checking an access key id and a secret access key. Think of them as your user name and password to gain access to Amazon S3.

You'll notice that the code we pasted in here doesn't actually HAVE the bucket name or the access key id or the secret access key listed. Why is that? Doesn't Amazon need to know those things?

Yes it does, but we don't want to type them in here. Why? Because sometimes people host their version control source files on Github.

Remember at the beginning of the book we chose to use BitBucket to host our version control because BitBucket is private and Github is public?

If you DID happen to use Github, all of your source code would be open for anyone to see...and if we typed in our Amazon secret keys here, people would be able to see them...and that's baaaad.

Rails gets around this problem by not making you type those things right here. Instead it uses environmental variables, designated by ENV['stuff here'], and those environmental variables keep your information secret.

We actually won't type in our bucket, access key, or secret key anywhere into our app, instead we'll type them directly into Heroku using a special command. Heroku will keep them on file, and whenever our program needs them, it will call the environmental variables which will then swap out the actual keys and codes from Heroku.

Confused? It's not too bad.

Before we type those three things into Heroku, we need to GET those three things. That means you need to log into Amazon AWS and find them. So let's do that now.

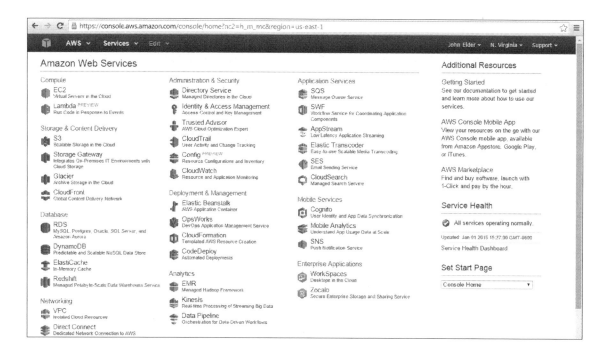

(Amazon AWS Console Screen)

Let's get our Bucket name first. From the Amazon Console, click the S3 link and then the "Create Bucket" link on the next screen.

(Amazon AWS Create Bucket Screen)

From the screen that pops up, name your bucket. A Bucket must be unique so keep trying till you pick a unique one...something like pinterested99 or some other number.

For region, select "US Standard" even if you're outside the US.

Next you'll be in the S3 bucket area, and you should see your newly created bucket. Now we need to set the permissions so that anyone can upload and view images in your bucket.

Right-click on your bucket name and select "properties" and a panel should pop up on the right-hand side of the screen. Next click on "Permissions", then click the little green plus sign to "add more permissions". Click the drop down box and select "Everyone", then click the tick marks next to all the listed permissions (list, upload/delete, view permissions, edit permissions).

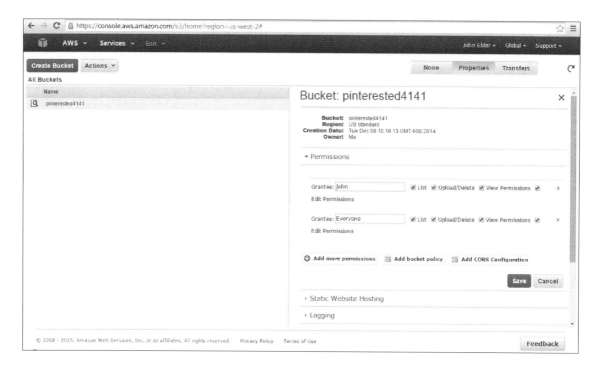

(Amazon AWS – Set Bucket Permissions)

Finally, click the "Save" button to save your new permissions. Your bucket is now ready to go, just remember the name (or write it down so you remember it).

OBTAINING AMAZON ACCESS AND SECRET KEYS

Now we just need to get a hold of an access key and secret key. If you just created a new Amazon AWS account, we'll need to do a couple of different things. If you're using an older AWS account that has already issued keys in the past, you can skip part of this.

If this is your first time...

Click on your name in the upper right-hand corner of the Amazon screen, and from the drop-down list that appears, select "Security Credentials".

Next, click on the "Create individual IAM users" link there in the middle of the screen. If you've already created an individual IAM user in the past, you don't have to do it again but I'm assuming this is your first time.

Click the "Manage Users" button that drops down.

On the next screen, click the big blue "Create New Users" button at the top of the screen.

Type in your name in one of the boxes, make sure the "generate access key for each user" box is clicked, then hit the blue "Create" button at the bottom of the page.

A screen will pop up saying that this is the last time you'll be able to get your secret key for this user, and there's a link that you can click to get the key. Click the link and copy the access key id and secret key. Save them somewhere.

Now you might think these are the access key id and secret access key that we need to enter into Heroku, but you'd be wrong.

For some reason we need to go through the whole process again to generate a new access key id and secret access key for our app. Don't ask me, I don't know why Amazon works the way it does…

Go ahead and click on your name at the top right-hand corner of the screen one more time, and select the "Security Credentials" link again.

This time, the screen that pops up will look a little different. I guess because it's no longer your first time…*shrugs*

If a box pops up asking you to either "Continue to Security Credentials" or "Get Started with IAM Users", select the security credentials option.

NOW, we'll see a link for "Access Keys (Access Key ID and Secret Access Key)" which is exactly what we want; click it.

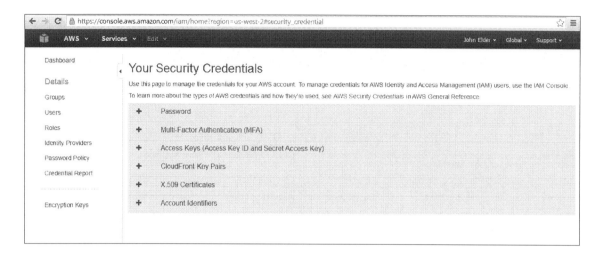

(Amazon AWS – Security Credentials Screen)

A sort of dropdown will appear with a big blue button that says "Create New Access Key"; click it.

A box should pop up telling you that your keys were created successfully. DON'T CLOSE THAT BOX!!

You only get one chance to write down your keys, and this is that one chance. You should see a little link at the bottom of that box that says something like: "Show Access Key"; click it and your keys will appear. Copy them and paste them into a notepad file or something.

Now it's time to add these guys to Heroku. There's a pretty good article about it right here:

https://devcenter.heroku.com/articles/paperclip-s3

You can read that if you want, but I'm going to walk you through it. All we need to do is tell Heroku what our bucket name is, our access key id, and our secret access key; and we've got all three of those so let's get right down to it:

```
1  $ heroku config:set S3_BUCKET_NAME=your_bucket_name
2  $ heroku config:set AWS_ACCESS_KEY_ID=your_access_key_id
3  $ heroku config:set AWS_SECRET_ACCESS_KEY=your_secret_access_key
4
```

Just replace the last little bit after the equal sign with your specific bucket name, access_key_id, and secret_access_key.

To make sure that Heroku got all that you can run this command:

```
1  $ heroku config
2
```

And it will spit out all the info it has stored about your app. If you've done everything correctly, you should see your bucket name, access key id, and secret access key.

So let's save all this work and push to heroku and see if it worked!

```
1  $ git add .
2  $ git commit –am 'integrated AmazonS3 with Heroku'
3  $ git push
4  $ git push heroku master
5  $ heroku run rake db:migrate
6
```

Now the moment of truth…head over to your heroku app, log in, and try to upload a pin. View the pin, is the image showing?

Right click on the image, and select "open image in new tab" to view the image itself. Take a look at the URL of the image after it's been opened in a new browser tab. Does the URL point to Amazon.com?

If so, everything went correctly. If not, something went wrong! But it should all be ok.

Congratulations! You're 90% done with your app! All we need to do now is add some jQuery touches and tinker with the look of our pins index page, and do a few more tiny odds and ends that won't be difficult at all…and we'll be done!

In the next chapter we'll start with the look and feel and I'll introduce you to jQuery Masonry…which is pretty cool.

CHAPTER EIGHT

STYLING WITH JQUERY MASONRY AND ADDING PAGINATION

We're nearing the end of our project! All we need to do is tinker with the look and feel of things, make some minor changes, and we'll be done.

Let's dive right in and get started!

First things first, our pins index page doesn't look like pinterest in any way shape or form. We need to change that pronto.

What we want is for each pin to be square/rectangular in form with the image on top, followed by the description below it. This sounds like a job for Bootstrap panels to me! But first we need to do some other stuff...

Right now our pins index page is dominated by that ugly table. Let's get rid of all traces of that table now, and we can get rid of the <h1> Listing pins</h1> tag too:

/app/views/pins/index.html.erb

```
1    <% @pins.each do |pin| %>
2      <%= image_tag pin.image.url(:medium) %>
3      <%= pin.description %>
4      <%= link_to 'Show', pin %>
5      <% if pin.user == current_user %>
6        <%= link_to 'Edit', edit_pin_path(pin) %>
7        <%= link_to 'Destroy', pin, method: :delete, data: { confirm: 'Are you
8      sure?' } %>
9      <% end %>
9    <% end %>
10  <br/>
11  <%= link_to 'New Pin', new_pin_path %>
12
```

I took out all traces of the table stuff. All the <td> and their corresponding </td> tags, all the <tr> tags…everything table related. It didn't leave us with much left!

Now let's add some line breaks to get things looking a little better:

/app/views/pins/index.html.erb

```
1      <% @pins.each do |pin| %>
3        <%= image_tag pin.image.url(:medium) %><br/>
5          <%= pin.description %><br/>
7
9          <%= link_to 'Show', pin %><br/>
10          <% if pin.user == current_user %>
11            <%= link_to 'Edit', edit_pin_path(pin) %><br/>
12            <%= link_to 'Destroy', pin, method: :delete, data: { confirm: 'Are you
13            sure?' } %><br/>
14          <% end %>
17        <% end %>
18        <br/>
19        <%= link_to 'New Pin', new_pin_path %>
20
```

(Pins Index Page Without Formatting)

And while we're at it, let's get rid of the "Show" link. Instead, let's make the image itself clickable. All we have to do is modify line 3 above (the image tag).

```
1  <%= link_to image_tag(pin.image.url(:medium)), pin %>
2
```

So now our pins index page looks like this:

/app/views/pins/index.html.erb

```
1     <% @pins.each do |pin| %>
2       <%= link_to image_tag(pin.image.url(:medium)), pin %><br/>
3         <%= pin.description %><br/>
4
5           <% if pin.user == current_user %>
```

```
6          <%= link_to 'Edit', edit_pin_path(pin) %><br/>
7          <%= link_to 'Destroy', pin, method: :delete, data: { confirm: 'Are you
8           sure?' } %><br/>
9         <% end %>
10        <br/>
11       <% end %>
12     <%= link_to 'New Pin', new_pin_path %>
13
```

So far so good; the pins look a little better, the only problem is that they scroll vertically down the page instead of horizontally across the page.

And when you resize the page, we want the pins to move around in a sort of animated way, just to add some cool effects to the site.

To do that, we're going to use something called jQuery Masonry. You can take a look at it at: http://masonry.desandro.com/

As like most things in Rails, Masonry comes as a Gem, so head over to RubyGems.org and search for masonry-rails and as of this book, the version number is 0.2.4, so go ahead and copy the reference and add it to your Gemfile. We'll also add jquery-turbolinks while we're at it.

Gemfile
```
1  .
2  .
3  gem 'jquery-turbolinks'
4  gem 'masonry-rails', '~> 0.2.4'
5
```

And as always, run bundle install to install it:

```
1  $ bundle install
2
```

While you're at RubyGems.org, click the "Documentation" link for Masonry and look through it, there's a few more steps to install this thing and they're precise.

Scroll down until you see the CSS Usage section:

/app/assets/stylesheets/application.css
```
1  .
2  .
3  *= require 'masonry/basic'
4  *= require 'masonry/centered'
5  *= require 'masonry/fluid'
6  *= require 'masonry/gutters'
7  *= require 'masonry/infinitescroll'
8  *= require 'masonry/right-to-left'
9  *= require 'masonry/transitions'
```

```
10  *= require_self
11   *= require_tree .
12  */
13
```

These app/assets/ files look a little different than other files we've played with so far. Take a look at line 10 and line 11 above. Basically line 11 tells our app to add all the files in this directory to our project, and line 10 tells our app to add this file to the project. So when we add things to that file, I like to put them above those two lines.

Let's look at all the things we just added (lines 3-9). Those are all the different things that Masonry will do. Notice the infinitescroll thing? You've probably seen that on websites before...

But actually, we don't need all of those things, we only need the transitions one. So let's update the file:

/app/assets/stylesheets/application.css

```
1  .
2  .
3  *= require 'masonry/transitions'
4  *= require_self
5  *= require_tree .
6  */
7
```

Looking through the Masonry documentation, we'll see that we also need to add a couple of lines to our Javascript manifest file as well:

/app/assets/javascripts/application.js

```
1  .
2  .
3  //= require jquery
4  //= require jquery.turbolinks
5  //= require jquery_ujs
6  //= require turbolinks
7  //= require bootstrap-sprockets
8  //= require bootstrap
9  //= require masonry/jquery.masonry
10  //= require_tree .
```

It's important to add the jquery.turbolinks reference directly below the jquery reference, otherwise things can get wonky and might not work.

Finally, we need to add a bit of CoffeeScript to our pins.js.coffee file:

/app/assets/javascripts/pins.js.coffee

```
1  # Place all the behaviors and hooks related to the matching controller here.
2  # All this logic will automatically be available in application.js.
3  # You can use CoffeeScript in this file: http://coffeescript.org/
4  $ ->
5    $('#pins').imagesLoaded ->
6      $('#pins').masonry
7        itemSelector: '.box'
8        isFitWidth: true
9
```

Finally, we've got to add a little bit of custom CSS to our CSS file:

/app/assets/stylesheets/pins.css.scss

```
1  // Place all the styles related to the pins controller here.
2  // They will automatically be included in application.css.
3  // You can use Sass (SCSS) here: http://sass-lang.com/
4
5  #pins {
6    margin: 0 auto;
7  }
8
9  .box {
10    margin: 5px;
11    width: 214px;
12  }
13
14  .box img {
15    width: 100%;
16  }
17
```

Strictly speaking, we could probably add that bit of CSS to our bootstraply.css.scss file, but since this code is going to style our pins, I put it in our pins.css.scss file.

That should take care of the setup for this thing, but now we need to configure our pins index page to actually use Masonry, and if you scroll down through the Masonry documentation, you'll see a section on 'Setup' that shows you how to call the divs and classes on your web page.

/app/views/pins/index.html.erb

```
1   <div id="pins" class="transitions-enabled">
2     <% @pins.each do |pin| %>
3   <div class="box">
4       <div class="panel panel-default">
5       <%= link_to image_tag(pin.image.url(:medium)), pin %><br/>
6       <div class="panel-body">
7         <%= pin.description %>
8       </div>
9
10      <div class="panel-footer">
11        <% if pin.user == current_user %>
12          <%= link_to 'Edit', edit_pin_path(pin) %>
13          <%= link_to 'Destroy', pin, method: :delete, data: { confirm: 'Are you
14          sure?' } %>
15        <% end %>
16      </div>
17    <% end %>
18
19    <%= link_to 'New Pin', new_pin_path %>
20      </div>
21    </div>
22  </div>
23
```

Basically all we're doing is (line 1) wrapping the entire page in a div with ID="pins" (which corresponds with the css we just added to our pins.css.scss file and as well as our pins.js.coffee file) and class=" transitions-enabled" (which tells masonry to do its transitions thing).

We're also (line 3) wrapping each individual pin in a div with class="boxy" which also corresponds with the css we just added to our pins.css.scss file as well as our pins.js.coffee file.

So if we restart our server and check out our website, our pins index page should scroll horizontally. And if we resize the screen, the pins should move about and resize with a cool animated transition effect.

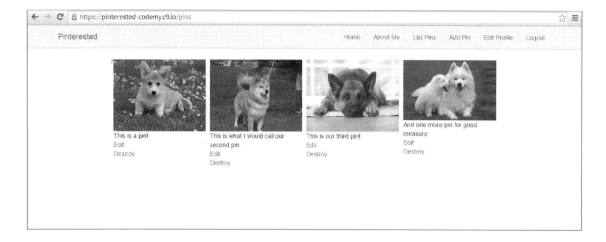

(Pins Index Page With Masonry Installed)

Now we can do the final step to make our pins look more like real Pinterest pins, and I think it's a perfect job for Bootstrap Panels:

/app/views/pins/index.html.erb

```
1  <div id="pins" class="transitions-enabled">
2    <% @pins.each do |pin| %>
3     <div class="box">
4      <div class="panel panel-default">
5      <%= link_to image_tag(pin.image.url(:medium)), pin %><br/>
6       <div class="panel-body">
7        <%= pin.description %><br/>
8       </div>
9        <% if pin.user == current_user %>
10        <div class="panel-footer">
11         <%= link_to 'Edit', edit_pin_path(pin) %><br/>
12         <%= link_to 'Destroy', pin, method: :delete, data: { confirm: 'Are you
13          sure?' } %>
14        </div>
15       <% end %>
16      </div>
17     </div>
18    <% end %>
19  </div>
20
```

You'll notice that I took out the link to "Add A New Pin" because we've got a link to that at the top of every page on the Navbar. Check it out:

(Pins Index Page With Panels)

You'll also notice that we've placed the "Edit" and "Destroy" links in a panel-footer that only shows up if a user is logged in and if they are the one who posted that specific pin. So if we log out and view the pins page, it will look like this:

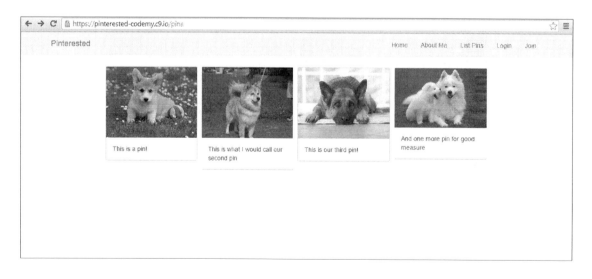

(Pins Index Page Not Logged In – No Panel Footer Links)

Basically at this point we can play around with the look and feel of these pins any way we like. I'll leave it to you to put your own spin on the final layout of your own app – have some fun with it!

TWEAKING PINS SHOW PAGE

Our pins index page looks pretty good, now let's edit our pins show page to look better:

/app/views/pins/show.html.erb

```
1
2  <div class="row">
3    <div class="col-md-offset-2 col-md-8">
4
5      <div class="panel panel-default">
6        <div class="panel-heading center"><%= image_tag @pin.image.url(:medium) %></div>
7        <div class="panel-body">
8
9          <%= @pin.description %><br/>
10
11          <% if @pin.user == current_user %>
12            <%= link_to 'Edit', edit_pin_path(@pin) %> |
13          <% end %>
14          <%= link_to 'Back', pins_path %>
15        </div>
16      </div>
17    </div>
18  </div>
19
```

The first thing I did was remove line one:

```
1   <p id="notice"><%= notice %></p>
2
```

I did that because we tweaked our pins controller a while back to output a flash message itself, so that line would result in two flash messages being shown at once and that's not cool.

Next, I wrapped the whole thing in a row div class because Bootstrap likes that, then I added line 3 to center things. Then I just wrapped the whole thing in a panel like we've done so many times in the past.

The layout is pretty simple, but gets the job done and I think we can call that done.

(Pins Show Page – Centered With Panels)

MAKING OUR SITE MOBILE FRIENDLY

These days your website has to be mobile friendly. Luckily for us, Bootstrap has taken care of all that for us. The only thing we have to do is add one single line to our layouts/application.html.erb file to tell the web browser that our site is mobile ready:

/app/views/layouts/application.html.erb

```
1  <!DOCTYPE html>
2  <html>
3  <head>
4    <title>Pinterested</title>
5    <%= stylesheet_link_tag    'application', media: 'all', 'data-turbolinks-track' => true %>
6    <%= javascript_include_tag 'application', 'data-turbolinks-track' => true %>
7    <%= csrf_meta_tags %>
8    <meta name="viewport" content="width=device-width, initial-scale=1, maximum-scale=1">
9
10  </head>
11  <body>
12  .
13  .
```

Line 8 is all we need to add to make our site mobile friendly. Now if you check out the site on a smart phone, you'll see that standard mobile dropdown menu at the top of the screen, and the site will resize to the size of your phone's screen.

Line 8 is a standard line of code that should go on every website you ever build, whether in Rails or otherwise.

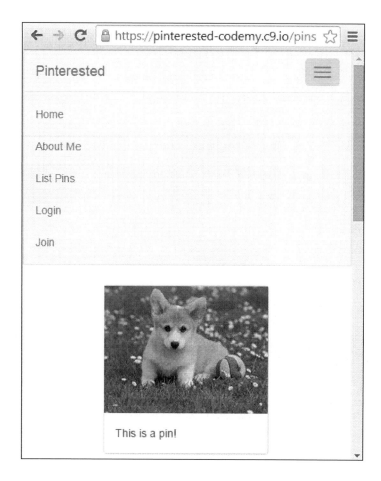

(Mobile Friendly Menu Dropdown)

REORDERING OUR PINS

Things are coming along nicely, we're almost finished! But we still have one small problem…and you may have noticed it yourself.

The pins on our pins index page are in the wrong order! Every time you add a new pin, it gets placed at the bottom of the list. Imagine if hundreds or thousands of pins were added. To see the newest one, you'd have to scroll down and down and down and down to see it.

We'd much rather have the newest pins listed at the very top of the page. Rails makes that very easy, all we have to do is edit out pins controller file a bit:

/app/controllers/pins_controller.rb

```
1  .
2  .
3  def index
4    @pins = Pin.all.order("created_at DESC")
5  end
6  .
7  .
8
```

We just slapped a ("created_at DESC") bit onto the end of our index controller. DESC stands for Descending…as opposed to Ascending. That just tells Rails to output our pins in descending order (newest to oldest).

That's all we have to do!

But it does beg the question…how many pins should we show on each page? We don't really want our pins index page to list thousands and thousands of pins, do we? Nope.

Instead, we should set some rules and break it up by only allowing so many pins to be shown on a page…say 20, or 50, or whatever you like.

We can do this by adding *pagination*.

As always…there's a Gem for that (or in this case, two Gems).

ADDING PAGINATION

We'll need two Gems to handle this, one to handle the actual Pagination, the other to tie Bootstrap into our Pagination so that we can use the cool looking Bootstrap Pagination classes.

/Gemfile
```
1  .
2  .
3  gem 'will_paginate', '~> 3.0.7'
4  gem 'will_paginate-bootstrap', '~> 1.0.1'
5
```

will_paginate handles the actual pagination stuff, and will_paginate-bootstrap ties our pagination into Bootstrap.

I'll leave you to look up each Gem at RubyGems.org and read the documentation. By now you should be pretty used to doing that.

To properly set up pagination, we need to make a couple of changes; one to our pins controller, and one to our pins index page. Let's look at the controller first:

/app/controllers/pins_controller.rb
```
1  .
2  .
3  def index
4     @pins = Pin.all.order("created_at DESC").paginate(:page => params[:page], :per_page => 3)
5  end
6  .
7  .
8
```

You'll remember how we just edited this file to output our pins in Descending order. Now we're tacking on a bit more to the end of that line. The only thing you need to take notice of is the '3' at the end of line 4.

That's where you choose how many pins to show per page. In our case, I've selected '3' because the pagination controls won't show up on the page unless there are as many pins as you've listed. By selecting '3', it means that the pagination will show up (since we have 4 pins and I'm too lazy to add more right now).

If this were a real commercial site that we intended to launch, I'd probably set it to 25 or 50.

Next we need to actually output our pagination onto the screen, so let's edit our pins index page:

/app/views/pins/index.html.erb
```
1  .
2  .
3  <%= will_paginate @posts %>
4
```

Just add that code to the very bottom of your pins index page. Be sure to restart your server (since we added new Gems). Let's check it out:

(Pins Index Page With Basic Pagination)

That's ok, but we'd rather style those pagination links better. Like I said, Bootstrap offers a pagination class. Head over to GetBootstrap.com and click the "Components" link, then the "Pagination" link to see the different options available.

Let's edit our pagination to incorporate Bootstrap:

/app/views/pins/index.html.erb

```
1  .
2  .
3  <%= will_paginate @pins, renderer: BootstrapPagination::Rails %>
4
```

Now reload the page and take a look:

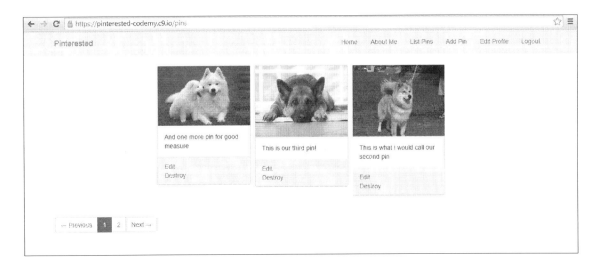

(Pins Index Page With Bootstraped Pagination)

Much better! But we should probably center the pagination in the middle of the screen. Let's add a center class to our bootstraply.css.scss file:

/app/assets/stylesheets/bootstraply.css.scss

```
1  .
2  .
3  @import "bootstrap-sprockets";
4  @import "bootstrap";
5
6  .center {
7    text-align: center;
8  }
9
```

Be sure to put our center class code UNDER the @import lines. Now we need to call that center class on our pins index page:

/app/views/pins/index.html.erb

1 .
2 .
3 <div class="center>
4   <%= will_paginate @pins, renderer: BootstrapPagination::Rails %>
5 </div>
6

Reload the page and it should look like this…

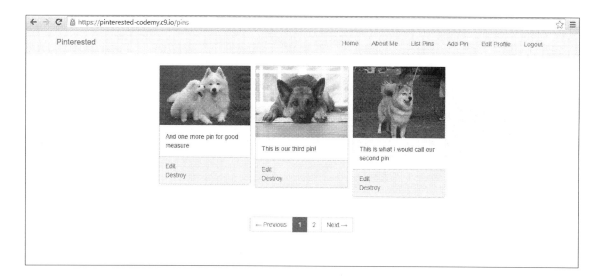

(Pins Index Page With Centered Bootstrap Pagination)

MAKING OUR PINS INDEX PAGE OUR HOMEPAGE

So this is great! Our pins index page looks like Pinterest, we've got pagination, and everything seems to be going our way.

Now it's time to make our pins index page our main homepage. Whenever someone comes to https://pinterested-codemy.c9.io (or whatever your URL is), we want our pins index page to be shown, not the homepage that we currently have (the one with the jumbotron).

If you like the jumbotron, you can always add it to your pins index page (maybe use a partial) and just use an IF statement to only show the jumbotron if a person is not logged in. But I'll leave that to you.

Right now I'm just going to make our pins index page our main homepage by changing the route.

/config/routes.rb
```
1  .
2  .
3  root 'pins#index'
4  .
5  .
6
```

All I did here was change our old root route from root 'home#index' to root 'pins#index'.

Now when someone goes to our site, the pins index page is the one they'll see.

Now let's save our work and push it up to Heroku.

```
1  $ git add .
2  $ git commit –am 'added masonry, pagination, and made pins our index page'
3  $ git push
4  $ git push heroku master
5
```

ADDING USER NAMES

Let's do one more thing before we end this project; let's tweak our entire project to allow people to add their names to their pins. This will allow us to pull a bunch of different things that we've learned together.

WARNING WARNING WARNING WARNING

Before we proceed, you need to delete all the pins that you've added so far, both on your development site as well as on Heroku. I know, it's a pain in the ass, but we're going to be tinkering with the database so just do it this one last time. You should also cancel your user account again just to be on the safe side.

We're going to need to tinker with our Users database table; right now it only records a user's email address and password, and we need to add a column to record their name as well. No problem, we've done that before when we added the user_id column to our pins table.

```
1  $ rails generate migration AddNameToUsers name:string
2
```

This is the command to add a "Name" column to our "Users" table. It looks a little different than the one we used earlier to add a User_ID column:

```
1  $ rails generate migration add_user_id_to_pins user_id:integer:index
2
```

In that command we used the underscore convention add_user_id_to_pins and in the command we just used to add Name, we used the camel case style of AddNameToUsers.

Either method works in Rails, and I wanted to point them both out to you – they both do the same thing.

Finally, notice that we designated 'name' to be a string data type.

Now we need to run our rake db:migrate command to push our new migration into the database (and be sure to run heroku run rake db:migrate later when you push all this up to Heroku):

```
1  rake db:migrate
2
```

Take a look at your database schema now, you should see a Name field in the Users table and it should be listed as a string.

Piece of cake! But now we need to update a couple of files so that people can actually type in their name when they sign up, and edit their name after they've signed up when they edit their user profile.

/app/views/devise/registrations/new.html.erb

```
1  .
2  .
3  <div class="form-group">
4    <%= f.label :name %>
5    <%= f.text_field :name, class: "form-control", :autofocus => true %>
6  </div>
7  .
8  .
```

/app/views/devise/registrations/edit.html.erb

```
1  .
2  .
3  <div class="form-group">
4    <%= f.label :name %>
5    <%= f.text_field :name, class: "form-control", :autofocus => true %>
6  </div>
7  .
8  .
```

This will add a form field and label to the new registration page so that people can add their name when they register, and also let people edit their name when they edit their user profile.

(https://pinterested-codemy.c9.io/users/sign_up With Name Field)

But we need to tell Rails that it's ok to accept a name from a web form, and we do that in the application controller.

/app/controllers/application_controller.rb

```
1   class ApplicationController < ActionController::Base
2     # Prevent CSRF attacks by raising an exception.
3     # For APIs, you may want to use :null_session instead.
4     protect_from_forgery with: :exception
5     before_filter :configure_permitted_parameters, if: :devise_controller?
6
7   protected
8
9    def configure_permitted_parameters
10     devise_parameter_sanitizer.for(:sign_up) << :name
11     devise_parameter_sanitizer.for(:account_update) << :name
12    end
13   end
14
```

And we also need to make a reference in our pin_params section of our pins controller:

/app/controllers/pins_controller.rb

```
1  .
2  def pin_params
3    params.require(:pin).permit(:description, :image, :name)
4  end
5  .
6  .
```

Just add that :name to the end of line 3. You'll see that this line already references description, and images…now we added name.

Now we just need to output each person's name under their particular pin in our pins index page and our pins show page:

/app/views/pins/index.html.erb

```
1  .
2  .
3  <%= link_to image_tag(pin.image.url(:medium)), pin %><br/>
4      <div class="panel-body">
5        <%= pin.description %><br/>
6        <br/><strong><%= pin.user.name if pin.user %></strong><br/>
7      </div>
8
```

And finally, let's update our pins show page to list the user's name as well:

/app/views/pins/show.html.erb

```
1  .
2  .
3  <%= @pin.description %><br/>
4  <br/><%= @pin.user.name %><br/>
5  .
6  .
7
```

Just add the reference to the name under the pin.description line and you should be good to go!

Now let's save our work:

```
1  $ git add .
2  $ git commit –am 'added user name, updated devise forms'
3  $ git push
4  $ git push heroku master
5  $ heroku run rake db:migrate
6
```

And that's all there is to it! That wasn't so bad.

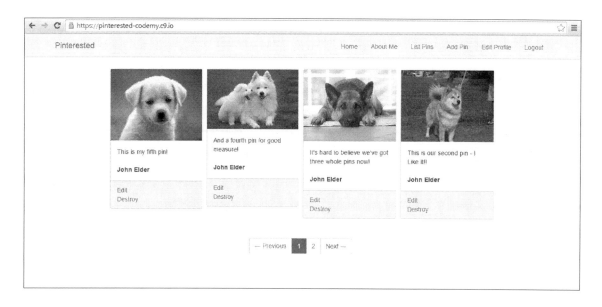

(https://pinterested-codemy.c9.io Index Page With User Names Added to Pins)

I think we're pretty much done with our app! All the major functionality exists, in the next chapter we'll make a few cosmetic changes to make the colors and whatnot look more like Pinterest...but for all intents and purposes – our site is done!

Congratulations on making it this far! You've accomplished something pretty incredible in a fairly short amount of time! Take a moment to appreciate it and we'll move along in the next chapter.

CHAPTER NINE

TWEAKING THE LOOK AND FEEL AND FINISHING UP

Our app is basically done, but we can play around with the look and feel a little bit to make it feel a little more pinteresty.

We talked about customizing bootstrap earlier in the book. Head over to GetBootstrap.com and click the "Customize" link to search through the different variables that you can play with.

There are really only a few minor changes I'd like to make.

First, I'd like to make the general theme color red, like at Pinterest. So I'd like the links on the site to be red; I'd like the buttons of the site to be red; and I'd like the title text on the Navbar to be red.

Specifically, I'd like to use this color of red: #cb2027;

Searching through the bootstrap customization variables, I see that links are controlled by:

```
1   $link-color: #cb2027;
2
```

And to change the title color of the Navbar to red we need:

```
1   $navbar-default-brand-color: #cb2027;
2
```

And finally, to change the colors of our buttons, we need to tweak the "primary" button color using this variable:

```
1  $brand-primary: #cb2027;
2
```

Next, I'd like to swap out the background color of our site and the Navbar background color.

I'd like our site's basic background color to be a light grey in color, and I'd like the Navbar to be white.

```
1  $body-bg: #e9e9e9;
2  $navbar-default-bg: #ffffff;
3
```

What else can we tinker with? How about the color of the pagination thing at the bottom of the screen; let's highlight that with the same red color:

```
1  $pagination-active-bg: #cb2027;
2  $pagination-active-border: #cb2027;
3
```

Let's see…why don't we tinker with the Navbar height and make it a little shorter:

```
1  $navbar-height: 40px;
2
```

Looking good! Now let's put all of these together on our bootstraply.css.scss file:

/app/assets/stylesheets/bootstraply.css.scss

```
1   $navbar-default-bg: #ffffff;
2   $navbar-height: 40px;
3   $body-bg: #e9e9e9;
4   $navbar-default-brand-color: #cb2027;
5   $link-color: #cb2027;
6   $pagination-active-bg: #cb2027;
7   $pagination-active-border: #cb2027;
8   $brand-primary: #cb2027;
9
10  @import "bootstrap-sprockets";
11  @import "bootstrap";
12
13  .center {
14      text-align: center;
15  }
16
```

And I think we'll call this thing finished! Remember to put the variables ABOVE the @import lines in the CSS file, and the actual CSS (like our center class) BELOW the @import lines.

Let's save our work one last time!

```
1   $ git add .
2   $ git commit –am 'tweaked bootstrap ui'
3   $ git push
4   $ git push heroku master
5
```

ADDING A CUSTOM URL

So our app is done, now let's add a custom URL to our heroku production app. We don't really want people coming to oursite.herokuapp.com when it could just as easily be oursite.com or custom.oursite.com

Creating a custom URL is pretty easy. If you don't have a domain name, purchase one at any domain registrar like godaddy.com or namecheap.com (either of those is good; domain names tend to cost around $10 bucks a year).

You have a couple of options, you can either point an actual domain name to your new Rails app, or you can point a sub-domain.

SUB-DOMAINS

I'll start out with a Sub-Domain because it's the easiest to explain. For our app, I want to use the sub-domain http://rails.codemy.com

So when someone goes to rails.codemy.com, I want our app to show up.

Easy as can be!

Just head over to Heroku, log in, then click on your app. On the screen that pops up, click the "Settings" link at the top of the screen.

Scroll down the screen and you'll see a section titled "Domains", click the "Edit" button in the Domains section.

A little form field should pop up where you can enter your sub-domain (or regular domain). So let's enter our:

rails.codemy.com

Click the little green plus sign after you type it in, then click the "Save" button.

What we've just done is tell Heroku that you'll be using rails.codemy.com as your apps URL. They just need a heads up.

Next, you'll need to log into your web host or domain registrar and create a CName that points to your heroku app URL (yourURL.herokuapp.com).

Every webhost and domain name registrar is different, so I can't really tell you how to do this step. You'll have to contact the support department of your specific host and ask them how to add a CName. It's usually pretty straight forward.

ADDING A CUSTOM DOMAIN

So that was how to add a sub-domain (rails.codemy.com) but how do you point a regular domain towards your app (like yoursite.com)??

It's the exact same process as before; log into Heroku, click "Settings" navigate down to the "Domains" section, and add your domain. But instead of typing in whatever.yoursite.com just type in yoursite.com

Note, you can't point www.yoursite.com to your app, it has to be yoursite.com (without the www).

Then like before, you need to contact your domain registrar and ask them how to add a CName to your domain. They'll tell you. Point that CName to your heroku URL (yourURL.herokuapp.com).

Heroku has an article about it that you can read if you're confused:

https://devcenter.heroku.com/articles/custom-domains

That's that!

CHAPTER TEN

CONCLUSION

You made it! We're done! Our app is finished, there's nothing left to do. I hope you enjoyed this book and got a lot out of it.

As cheesy as it may sound, I also hope you discovered a joy for Rails. It really is a great tool for building very professional websites, very quickly and easily. Think about our own app…

When you get right down to it, there wasn't more than a couple of hours of work involved in building this thing.

Sure it probably took longer than a couple hours the first time through while you were reading the book and learning…but the actual steps involved (once you learned them), didn't take much actual time to accomplish.

And we've got a pretty impressive site. People can sign up, sign in, sign out, update their profiles, add pins (CRUD!) and Rails handles all of that stuff behind the scenes for us.

That's a pretty professional set of functions and it was really pretty easy to do. That's the power of Rails.

You've taken a huge first step in Learning Rails, but there's so much more to learn. I hope you'll keep at it!

I also recommend that you head over to **Codemy.com** and check out some of my other Rails courses. I build all kinds of different sites in the different courses, and they're all a lot of fun.

You can take individual courses at Codemy.com for $39 each, or you can sign up for all the courses listed (and all future courses that we release) for just $99.

If you sign up today for all the courses, I'll give you a coupon code worth $20 off…you pay just $79…which is a tremendous deal. Watch over my shoulder as I build all kinds of sites in Rails (and other programming languages too) and talk you through it all step by step.

Just use coupon code rails101 at checkout to get the special $79 price tag.

See you there!

-John Elder
Codemy.com

APPENDIX A

SPECIAL CODEMY.COM OFFER

Learning never stops, especially for coders. There's always something new and cool to learn. I've tried to build a website that makes it super easy to learn how to code, and learn new coding skills...and it's called Codemy.com

Each course at Codemy.com is a series of videos where you watch over my shoulder as I build something cool (like this pinterested project we just created in this book).

In one course I build a Twitter-like site where people can post anonymous secrets. In other course I build a social network for people looking to start bands. In another course I build an affiliate marketing site that makes money from Amazon affiliate products.

I teach Rails courses, PHP courses, HTML and CSS courses, and more.

Each course costs $97, or you can sign up for all the courses for $497 (which is a pretty good deal if you ask me!) and that entitles you to all the future courses that we add absolutely free (and we've got some cool courses on the horizon).

AS A SPECIAL THANK YOU FOR READING THIS BOOK...

I'd love to see you over at Codemy.com and I'd like to bribe you to join today; so I'm giving you a special coupon code (**amazon**) that will give you $22 off my Ruby on Rails For Web Development course (so you pay $75 instead of $97)...

It's my gift to you! **http://www.Codemy.com/rails/**

So you get access to my best-selling course and for just **$75** instead of the regular $97.

And we offer a two month-long 100% money back guarantee. Check out the course, if it isn't for you…just shoot me a message and I'll immediately refund your money, no questions asked, no hoops to jump through.

HANDS ON HELP

Membership doesn't just get you videos…you also get hands on help from me and other members. Any time you get stuck with something, you can post a question to me directly, or post a question in our members forum.

It's a great resource and I hope you'll take advantage of it.

Just use coupon code **amazon** at checkout for $22 off my Ruby on Rails For Web Development course **http://www.Codemy.com/rails/**

See you on the inside!

-John Elder
Codemy.com

THE END

NOTES

NOTES

<u>NOTES</u>